INDONESIAN PHRASEBOOK

Patrick Witton

Indonesian Phrasebook
4th edition – November 2000
First published – June 1984

Published by
Lonely Planet Publications, Pty Ltd ABN 36 005 607 983

Lonely Planet Offices
Australia PO Box 617, Hawthorn, Victoria 3122
USA 150 Linden St, Oakland CA 94607
UK 10a Spring Place, London NW5 3BH
France 1 rue du Dahomey, 75011 Paris

Cover illustration
Gamelan Jammin' by Julian Chapple

ISBN 0 86442 651 8

Printed by The Bookmaker International Ltd
Printed in China

About the Author

Patrick's interest in Indonesian was born out of necessity, when he found himself lost in a Yogyakarta market at the age of 12. He has since studied the language both in Melbourne and at IKIP Bandung, under the Darmasiswa scholarship scheme. He currently works as an editor and author of Lonely Planet's *World Food* series.

From the Author

A squillion thanks go to Rudiat Komara and Ayuning Budiati, to Asti Mulyana and Dwi Muliati (as well as their families), to Kylie Nam and Andrew Taylor, to Rufin Kedang and Lily Djajamihardja, to Ron Witton for getting me started, and to Rachel Blake for sharing her ideas and appetite.

From the Publisher

This book was put together thanks to design and layout man Patrick Marris, illustrator Jules Chapple, who also drew the cover, editor Vicki Webb and cartographer Natasha Velleley. Rufin Kedang and Sally Steward proofread, Fabrice Rocher and Peter D'Onghia checked the layout and Karin Vidstrup Monk saw that it all ran smoothly.

Thanks to Paul Woods, Kristiana Sarwo Rini and Margit Meinhold who wrote previous editions of the Lonely Planet *Indonesian phrasebook*, from which this edition was developed.

CONTENTS

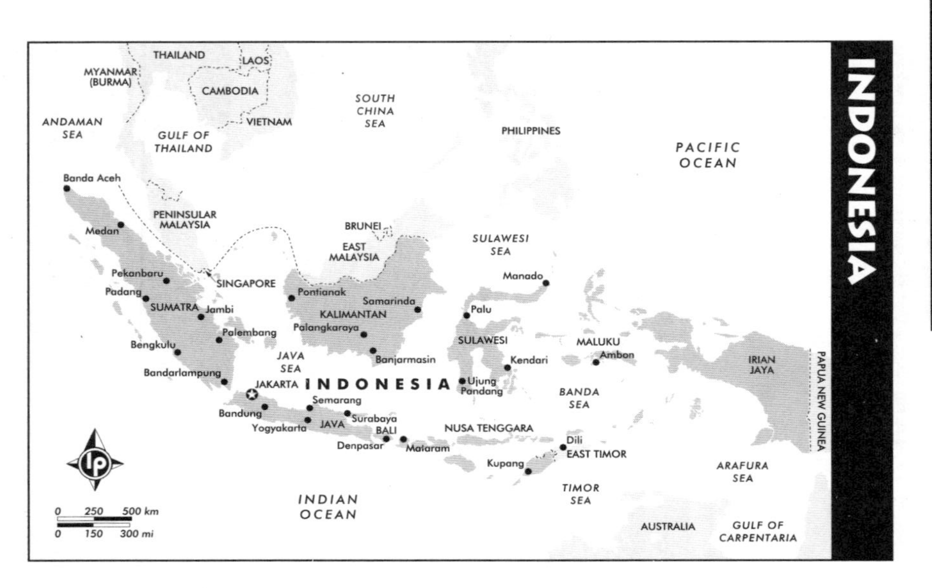
INDONESIA
THAILAND
LAOS
MYANMAR (BURMA)
CAMBODIA
SOUTH CHINA SEA
ANDAMAN SEA
VIETNAM
GULF OF THAILAND
PHILIPPINES
PACIFIC OCEAN
Banda Aceh
PENINSULAR MALAYSIA
Medan
BRUNEI
EAST MALAYSIA
SULAWESI SEA
Pekanbaru
SINGAPORE
Manado
Padang
Pontianak
SUMATRA
Jambi
Samarinda
KALIMANTAN
Palu
Palembang
Palangkaraya
SULAWESI
MALUKU
Bengkulu
JAVA SEA
Banjarmasin
Kendari
Ambon
IRIAN JAYA
Bandarlampung
JAKARTA
INDONESIA
Ujung Pandang
BANDA SEA
Semarang
Bandung
Surabaya
Yogyakarta
JAVA
BALI
NUSA TENGGARA
Denpasar
Mataram
Dili
EAST TIMOR
PAPUA NEW GUINEA
Kupang
ARAFURA SEA
INDIAN OCEAN
TIMOR SEA
0 250 500 km
0 150 300 mi
AUSTRALIA
GULF OF CARPENTARIA

INTRODUCTION

Welcome to Indonesia – 13,000 islands, 300 distinct cultural groups and indigenous languages, and one language, Bahasa Indonesia (Indonesian), understood right across the archipelago. From Sabang in the west to Merauke in the east, local linguistic differences can be as diverse as those found across Europe or Africa.

However, while there's no one language that's understood throughout Europe or Africa, there is an Indonesian language that bridges the communication divide. Indonesian has grown to become the lingua franca of this cultural farrago ever since President Sukarno and Vice President Mohammed Hatta used Indonesian to write the Declaration of Indonesian Independence in August 1945.

It's not as if other languages have died out – in fact Indonesian remains a second language to most. But Indonesian is the language used every day between Sundanese, Javanese, Sumbawans, Makassarese and Floresians when they share bus seats in Denpasar, offices in Bandung and food-stall benches in Pontianak.

For you the visitor, learning even the basics of Indonesian will change a good holiday into an unforgettable experience. Instead of observing happenings from a muted distance you'll be in there hunting through laneways, buying tickets to Tasikmalaya, learning the right way to eat a salak. What's more, your attempt to use Indonesian – no matter how slow or stuttered – will be met with enthusiasm and appreciation.

Indonesian is a living language. Spend time skimming newspapers and deciphering graffiti and you'll notice foreign words that have been readily adopted into Indonesian. Words like demokrasi 'democracy' and korupsi 'corruption' are a part of everyday speech. But this continuous influx of words was not borne of the information superhighway. Indonesian is a Malay-based language, which itself has adopted words and concepts through both slow evolution and a history of lively trade. There are links in Indonesian to languages such as Sanskrit (istana, palace), Arabic (hakim, judge), Portuguese (meja, table), Chinese (mie, noodle), Dutch (kantor, office) and English (otomatis, automatic). But the flow hasn't all been one way. Take for example the English word 'orangutan', derived from the Indonesian orang hutan (lit: forest person), also 'cockatoo' from kakatua, and the phrase 'to run amok', which comes from the verb of the same meaning, mengamuk. It's interesting to note that both Indonesians and some northern Australian Aborigines call white people blanda

It's said that Indonesian is easy to learn but takes a lifetime to master. Indeed the language is home to infinite irregularities and broken rules, as well as a surfeit of affixes. On top of this, people take short cuts when talking, they make up words, mix it with Bahasa Daerah, 'local languages', and mumble.

But for the beginner, Indonesian offers phonetic spelling, genderless grammar, tense-friendly structure and a user-friendly environment. You can easily get by without using the many prefixes and suffixes (in fact Indonesians often simplify their word usage when speaking) and people will often slow down their speech to your pace.

Even if you have to say:

> Ma'af, saya belum lancar dalam Bahasa Indonesia.
> Sorry, I'm not fluent in Indonesian yet.

on a regular basis, you'll find that with a few words, your independence and enjoyment is greatly enhanced. So as there's nothing to lose – maju terus jangan mundur, 'go for it, don't back down'.

TO YOU & YOU & YOU

Throughout this book, the polite pronoun Anda is used, but it can be replaced with the informal mu and kau, or the respectful bapak or ibu (see Grammar, pages 22-24), depending on the situation. No matter what pronoun is used, the sentence structure won't change.

ABBREVIATIONS IN THIS BOOK

adj	adjective
col	colloquial
excl	exclusive
f	feminine
incl	inclusive
lit	literal
m	masculine
n	noun
pl	plural
pol	polite
resp	respectful
v	verb

HOW TO USE THIS PHRASEBOOK

You *Can* Speak Another Language

It's true – anyone can speak another language. Don't worry if you haven't studied languages before, or that you studied a language at school for years and can't remember any of it. It doesn't even matter if you failed English grammar. After all, that's never affected your ability to speak English! And this is the key to picking up a language in another country. You don't need to sit down and memorise endless grammatical details and you don't need to memorise long lists of vocabulary. You just need to start speaking. Once you start, you'll be amazed how many prompts you'll get to help you build on those first words. You'll hear people speaking, pick up sounds from TV, catch a word or two that you think you know from the local radio, see something on a billboard – all these things help to build your understanding.

Plunge In

There's just one thing you need to start speaking another language – courage. Your biggest hurdle is overcoming the fear of saying aloud what may seem to you to be just a bunch of sounds.

The best way to start overcoming your fear is to memorise a few key words. These are the words you know you'll be saying again and again, like 'hello', 'thank you' and 'how much?'. Here's an important hint though: right from the beginning, learn at least one phrase that will be useful but not essential. Such as 'good morning' or 'good afternoon', 'see you later' or even a conversational piece like 'lovely day, isn't it?' or 'it's cold today' (people everywhere love to talk about the weather). Having this extra phrase (just start with one, if you like, and learn to say it really well) will enable you to move away from the basics, and when you get a reply and a smile, it'll also boost your confidence. You'll find that people you speak to will like it too, as they'll understand that at least you've tried to learn more of the language than just the usual essential words.

Ways to Remember

There are several ways to learn a language. Most people find they learn from a variety of these, although people usually have a preferred way to remember. Some like to see the written word and remember the sound from what they see. Some like to just hear it spoken in context (if this is you, try talking to yourself in Indonesian, but do it in the car or somewhere private, to give yourself confidence, and so others don't wonder about your sanity!). Others, especially the more mathematically inclined, like to analyse the grammar of a language, and piece together words according to the rules of grammar. The very visually inclined like to associate the written word and even sounds with some visual stimulus, such as from illustrations, TV and general things they see in the street. As you learn, you'll discover what works best for you – be aware of what made you really remember a particular word, and if it sticks in your mind, keep using that method.

Kicking Off

Chances are you'll want to learn some of the language before you go. The first thing to do is to memorise those essential phrases and words. Check out the basics (pages 39-40) ... and don't forget that extra phrase (see Plunge In!, page 12). Try the sections on making conversation or greeting people for a phrase you'd like to use. Write some of these words down on a separate piece of paper and stick them up around the place. On the fridge, by the bed, on your computer, as a bookmark – somewhere where you'll see them often. Try putting some words in context – the 'How much is it?' note, for instance, could go in your wallet.

CLEANING UP

In 1972, both the Indonesian and Malaysian governments decided to uniform the spelling of Bahasa Indonesia and Bahasa Malaysia, to simplify and phase out colonial influence within their languages. It was at this time that the orthography 'tj' became 'c', 'dj' became 'j' and 'j' became 'y'. In 1948, 'oe' became 'u'. You will, however, see the old spelling used in people's names as well as in alternative spelling for placenames.

OLD SPELLING	MODERN SPELLING
Soeharto	Suharto (the former President)
Tjiandjoer	Cianjur (a town in West Java)
Djokdjakarta	Yogyakarta (the capital)

Building the Picture

We include a chapter on grammar in our books for two reasons.

Firstly, some people have an aptitude for grammar and find understanding it a key tool to their learning. If you're such a person, then the grammar chapter will help you build a picture of the language, as it works through all the basics.

The second reason for the grammar chapter is that it gives answers to questions you might raise as you hear or memorise some key phrases. You may find a particular word is always used when there is a question – check out the grammar heading on questions and it should explain why. This way you don't have to read the grammar chapter from start to finish, nor do you need to memorise a grammatical point. It will simply present itself to you in the course of your learning. Key grammatical points are repeated throughout the book.

Any Questions?

Try to learn the main question words (see page 14). As you read through different situations, you'll see these words used in the example sentences, and this will help you remember them. So if you want to hire a bicycle, turn to the Bicycles section in Getting Around (use the Contents or Index pages to find it quickly). You've already tried to memorise the word for 'where' and you'll see the word for 'bicycle'. When you come across the sentence 'Where can I hire a bicycle?', you'll recognise the key words and this will help you remember the whole phrase. If there's no category for your need, try the dictionary (the question words are repeated there too, with examples), and memorise the phrases 'Please write that down' and 'How do you say ...?' (see page 58).

INDONESIAN & MALAYSIAN

Although the national languages of Indonesia and Malaysia are both based on the same language known as Malay, the languages have diverged and are developing in somewhat different directions. Many traditional Malay words are falling out of use in Indonesia and are being replaced or supplemented by new words borrowed from Javanese and English, among other sources.

You'll find, however, that your knowledge of Bahasa Indonesia will form a good basis for travelling in and learning the language of Malaysia.The structures and grammars remain common to both languages – the differences lie in vocabulary. Unfortunately, these differences in vocabulary include many of the most commonly used words.

In most cases, your Bahasa Indonesia used in Malaysia will be well understood and will probably just be considered a source of amusement. The following are some of the most prominent differences between modern Bahasa Malaysia and Bahasa Indonesia. Although many of these differences aren't reflected in dictionaries, they're in common usage.

English	Indonesian	Malaysian
after	sesudah	*selepas*
afternoon	sore	*petang*
always	selalu	*senantiasa*
beef	daging sapi	*daging lembu*
brother	kakak/laki-laki	*abang*
car	mobil	*kereta*
city	kota	*bandar*
cold (adj)	dingin	*sejuk*
cute (of baby)	lucu	*manis*
delicious	enak	*sedap*
to invite	mengundang	*menjemput*
Mr	Bapak	*Tuan*
Mrs	Ibu	*Puan*

office	kantor	*pejabat*
petrol	bensin	*petrol*
to return	kembali	*balik*
room	kamar	*bilik*
shoes	sepatu	*kasut*
shop	toko	*kedai*
soon	sebentar	*sekejap*
staff	pegawai	*kakitangan*
Sunday	Hari Minggu	*Hari Ahad*
toilet	WC; kamar kecil	*tandas*

I've Got a Flat Tyre

Doesn't seem like the phrase you're going to need? Well in fact, it could be very useful. As are all the phrases in this book, provided you have the courage to mix and match them. We have given specific examples within each section. But the key words remain the same even when the situation changes. So while you may not be planning on any cycling during your trip, the first part of the phrase 'I've got ...' could refer to anything else, and there are plenty of words in the dictionary that, we hope, will fit your needs. So whether it's 'a ticket', 'a visa' or 'a condom', you'll be able to put the words together to convey your meaning.

Finally

Don't be concerned if you feel you can't memorise words. On the inside front and back covers are the most essential words and phrases. You could also try tagging a few pages for other key phrases, or use the notes pages to write your own reminders.

PRONUNCIATION

Indonesian is written as it's spoken in Roman script, so learning correct pronunciation isn't an arduous exercise.

The Javanese are said to speak at the speed of a snail, markedly different to the firecracker pace of the Sumatrans. As with all stereotypes, there are exceptions, but you'll notice these variations in pace as you travel.

Indonesians are often quick to commend, but reluctant to correct. A good way to learn proper pronunciation is to ask an Indonesian who's staying or working at your hotel to run through a few words with you. This is an effective way to clear up mistakes before they become habitual.

RAISING THE TONE

Compared with English, Indonesian is rather monotone, with a slow rise of pitch toward the end of a sentence being the only noticeable change in tone.

VOWELS

a — as the 'a' in Julie Andrews' 'do-re-me-*fa*'. The 'a' in 'bat' is never found in Indonesian.
e — when stressed, as the 'e' in 'bet'; when unstressed, as the 'a' in 'about'
i — as the 'i' in 'unique'
o — at the end of a syllable, as the 'o' in 'hot'; elsewhere, as the the 'o' in 'for'
u — as the 'oo' in 'book'

Diphthongs

Indonesian has three vowel combinations:

ai — as the 'y' in 'fly', but more drawn out
au — as the 'ow' in 'cow', but more drawn out
ua — as the 'oo' in 'too' + the 'a' in 'father', with a slight 'w' sound in between

CONSONANTS

Consonants in Indonesian are pronounced as they are in English, with the following exceptions:

b	at the end of a word, as the 'b' in 'rub' (almost a 'p' sound); elsewhere, pronounced more strongly, as the 'b' in 'better'
k	at the end of a word, a glottal stop – the sound made between the words 'uh-oh'; elsewhere, as the 'k' in 'king'
g	always pronounced hard, as the 'g' in 'goat', never as the 'j' in 'joke'
'	glottal stop. The sound made between the words 'uh-oh'.
h	always pronounced. Stressed a little more strongly than in English, as if you were sighing. This heavy pronunciation is particularly evident for words of Arabic origin, when the 'h' appears between two vowels that are the same.
c	as the 'ch' in 'chair', never as the 'c' in 'cable' or the 'c' in 'cedar'
j	as the 'j' in 'join'
ng	always pronounced as the 'ng' in 'sing'. If followed by another 'g', the second 'g' is pronounced, giving a sound as the 'ng' in 'anger'.
ny	as the 'ny' in 'canyon'
r	always trilled clearly and distinctly
sy	as the word 'she' + the 'a' in 'father'

STRESS

Stress falls on the second-last syllable of a word. Therefore, with two-syllable words, the first syllable is stressed.

bagus	*ba*-goos	great

There are many aspects of Indonesian grammar that make it an easy language to learn. For example, nouns don't have to have plural forms, and verbs don't change according to their subject or tense.

Of course, Indonesian is susceptible to the idiosyncrasies that lace any language, and to claim that you'll speak fluently in five easy steps would be somewhat misleading. But for the purpose of basic communication, Indonesian grammar is both logical and easily grasped.

GRAMMATICAL TERMS

A number of terms are used in this chapter. The term 'subject' refers to the noun which governs the verb. With a sentence such as 'The woman is washing the dog', 'the woman' is the subject, as she is 'washing'. The 'object' is a noun that is affected by the verb – in this case, the dog.

The term 'possessive' is applied to a noun or a pronoun that's in a possessive relationship with a noun, as in 'your book'.

ROOT WORDS

Indonesian uses a series of 'root words' – base words to which prefixes and suffixes are added to create new words, such as verbs and nouns. Some transitions follow a logical system, such as:

senang	happy
kesenangan	happiness
menyenangkan	to make someone happy; enjoyable

Others are more cryptic:

duduk	sit
penduduk	population
menduduki	to occupy (a country)

You can create a noun from many root words by adding the suffix -an to the root.

Root Word		Noun	
bite	gigit	a bite	gigit*an*
swing	buai	a hammock	buai*an*

To create verbs, a prefix and/or a suffix may be added, depending on the type of verb (see page 29). For example, many common verbs have exactly the same form as the root word, while others take either the prefix ber- or me(n)-

Root Word		Verb	
go	pergi	to go	pergi
play	main	to play	*ber*main
answer	jawab	to answer	*men*jawab

Other affixes include memper-, di-, -i and -kan

Root Word		Verb	
word	kata	to talk about	*memper*kata*kan*
word	kata	to speak	*ber*kata
word	kata	to be said	*di*kata*kan*

WORD ORDER

The word order for Indonesian sentences is the same as in English – subject, verb, object.

I am reading a book.	Saya membaca buku. (lit: I to-read book)

However, it's quite common in Indonesian for the object to be mentioned first if it's being stressed. As this requires modification of the verb form, it's easier as a beginner to simply use the subject-verb-object construction.

ARTICLES

Instead of using a definite article like 'the' in English, Indonesian uses the demonstrative pronouns ini 'this/these' and itu 'that/those' when speaking of a specific object.

that red hat	topi merah itu (lit: hat red that)

The suffix -nya is also used the same way that English speakers use the definite article 'the'.

I'm going to the office.	Saya ke kantor*nya*. (lit: I to office-the)

(See page 25 for other uses of -nya.)

NOUNS

Plurals

This is one area where Indonesian shows itself to be user friendly. If you want to indicate that there's more than one of something, just say that thing twice.

child	anak	children	anak-anak

More often than not, you won't even need to repeat the noun, as context will indicate whether something is plural. For example, if you're buying a kilo of bananas, you'd ask for sekilo pisang (lit: a-kilo banana), not sekilo pisang-pisang, 'a-kilo bananas'.

PRONOUNS

Personal Pronouns

Indonesian personal pronouns can be a little confusing, as Indonesians will often use a person's name, family status, or title instead of the pronouns 'I' or 'you'.

Indonesians tend to use their own names or titles when referring to ythemselves, rather than using 'I'. This it may take a while getting used to someone named 'Rudy' saying:

Rudy ngantuk. (lit: Rudy sleepy)	Rudy is sleepy.

when the sense is:

Saya ngantuk. (lit: I sleepy)	I'm sleepy.

SG	I		saya/aku/gua
	you	(inf)	kamu/engkau (shortened to mu/kau)
		(pol)	Anda/saudara
		(resp, m)	bapak
		(resp, f)	ibu
	he		dia
	she		dia
PL	we	(incl)	kita
		(excl)	kami
	you	(pl)	kalian
	they		mereka

The pronoun 'you' has always posed a problem for learners of Indonesian, as an across-the-board 'you' doesn't exist. There are several forms, which range in their level of politeness.

Probably the safest form of 'you' to use is one of the following:

bapak	sir
ibu	ma'am

These are respectful terms of address often used for older men or women, but they can also be used to address anyone except the very young.

Other terms that can be used for 'you' include:

mbak	(lit: older sister) used for younger women; a Javanese term
mas	(lit: older brother) used for younger men; a Javanese term
adik	(lit: younger brother/sister) used for children

COMMON LEARNER'S MISTAKES

- In Indonesian, there are two ways to translate the English word 'for'.

  When you want to say 'on behalf of', 'for the purpose of' or 'intended or destined for', use **untuk**.

This drink is for you.	**Minum ini untuk Anda.** (lit: drink this for you)

  When describing a period of time, use **selama**.

I'm here for three days.	**Saya di sini selama tiga hari.** (lit: I at here for three day)

- Non-native speakers regularly interchange the verbs **melihat**, 'to look' and **menonton**, 'to watch'.

I can see him.	**Saya bisa melihat dia.** (lit: I can look him)
I'm watching television.	**Saya menonton tv.** (lit: I watch television)

Throughout this book, the polite pronoun Anda is used, but it can be replaced with mu, kalian, bapak or ibu depending on the situation. No matter what pronoun is used, the sentence structure won't change.

SG	my your (pol) his/her	saya Anda -nya
PL	our (inc/excl) your their	kita/kami kalian mereka/-nya

There's no equivalent in Indonesian for the English pronoun 'it' – either a noun or the pronoun itu, 'that', is used instead.

It is here. Itu di sini. (lit: that here)

The first person plural 'we' has two versions:

kita inclusive – includes the person being spoken to
kami exclusive – excludes the person being spoken to

POSSESSION

The possessive pronouns 'my, your, our, their' have the same form as the personal pronouns, and are placed after the thing that's possessed.

my jacket jaket saya (lit: jacket my)

In the third person singular (he, she), the suffix -nya (lit: of-him/her) is added to the thing that's possessed.

his jacket	jaket*nya* (lit: jacket-of-him)

The suffix -nya can also be used in place of the plural possessive pronoun mereka, 'their'.

their house	rumah*nya* (lit: house-of-them)
their house	rumah mereka (lit: house their)

ADJECTIVES

Adjectives always come after the word they're describing.

red book	buku merah (lit: book red)
big book	buku besar (lit: book big)

The pronoun yang, 'which/who', is often used with an adjective, especially when describing more than one thing about the noun.

the small, red book	buku merah yang kecil (lit: book red which small)
the big, white house	rumah putih yang besar (lit: house white which big)

Comparatives

Comparisons are made with the use of either lebih 'more' or kurang 'less', which are placed before the adjective. The word daripada, 'than', appears after the adjective to form the following construction:

lebih/kurang + adj + daripada (lit: more/less ... than)

bigger than ...	**lebih besar daripada ...** (lit: more big than)
smaller than ...	**lebih kecil daripada ...** (lit: more small than)

Daripada is also used if both objects being compared are mentioned.

Mangoes are more expensive than bananas.
Mangga lebih mahal daripada pisang.
(lit: mango more expensive than banana)

Comparisons of equality indicated in English by the phrase 'as ... as' are indicated in Indonesian by the prefix **se-**.

as big as	**sebesar** (lit: se-big)
as expensive as	**semahal** (lit: se-expensive)

GRAMMAR

THE MORE THINGS CHANGE

As well as introducing new rules to the Indonesian spelling system (see page 13), it was decided that words that include a preposition should become two words, with the preposition separated.

Old Spelling	New Spelling
disini	di sini (lit: at here)
kesana	ke sana (lit: to there)
darimana	dari mana (lit: from where)

It was also decided that the pronoun **Anda**, 'you' should be spelled with a capital 'A', as with 'Sie' in German.

Superlatives

To indicate extremes of comparison, yang paling (lit: which most) is used in the following construction:

noun + yang paling + adj

the biggest shop	toko yang paling besar (lit: shop which most big)
the most expensive	yang paling mahal (lit: which most expensive)

ADVERBS

As in English, adverbs can appear at the beginning, end or within a sentence.

COMMON ADVERBS

also	juga
always	selalu
here	di sini
immediately	segera
maybe	mungkin
never	tidak pernah
not yet	belum
often	sering
perhaps	barangkali; bisa jadi
possible	mungkin
rarely	jarang
sometimes	kadang-kadang
there	di sana
there (nearby)	di situ
too (also)	juga
too (big, small, etc)	terlalu
very	sekali/sangat

They often holiday in Bali.	Mereka sering berlibur di Bali. (lit: they often to-holiday at Bali)
I'll depart immediately.	Saya berangkat segera. (lit: I depart immediately)

CLASSIFIERS

Indonesian has an abundance of classifiers, or 'measure words', used when talking about quantities of nouns. There are many such words in English, as in 'two *pairs* of pants', 'four *slices* of cake', 'ten *sheets* of paper'.

In Indonesian, it's not imperative to use a classifier in everyday speech, but if you do, the most common are:

- ekor — used for animals

  There are three dogs. — Ada tiga ekor anjing. (lit: there-are three ekor dog)

- buah — used for inanimate objects

  There are five books. — Ada lima buah buku. (lit: there-are five buah book)

- orang — used for people

  There are three teachers. — Ada empat orang guru. (lit: there-are three orang teacher)

Classifiers are most frequently used when speaking about only *one* person or thing. Satu, 'one', becomes se- and is placed in front of the classifier.

one dog	*se*ekor anjing (lit: one-ekor dog)
one book	*se*buah buku (lit: one-buah book)
one teacher	*se*orang guru (lit: one-orang teacher)

VERBS

Verbs don't change according to subject or tense. They're formed from root-words, to which prefixes and/or suffixes may be added, depending on the type of verb. However, the bare root-word form can always be used in everyday speech and you'll still be understood.

Even if you don't use affixes yourself, you'll no doubt notice Indonesian speakers adding them to root-words. The correct prefix or suffix depends on the type of verb and its context in a sentence.

SIT-SIT

Doubling some verbs and adjectives alters their meaning.

to sit	duduk	sitting around	duduk-duduk
slow	pelan	slowly	pelan-pelan

Types of Verbs

Although Indonesian has several types of verbs, there are three main verb-types that you'll hear frequently.

1. The simplest type stands alone and never requires a prefix. Fortunately, many of the most commonly used verbs fit into this category:

to bathe	mandi	to go	pergi
to drink	minum	to sit	duduk
to eat	makan	to sleep	tidur

2. The second type is the ber- verb, with ber- being the prefix to the root-word.

For example, the root-word tanya, 'ask', becomes bertanya, 'to ask'. If the root-word starts with r, such as renang 'swim', the prefix drops the r and the verb becomes berenang 'to swim'.

Root Word		Verb	
say	kata	to say	berkata
play	main	to play	bermain

3. The third type of verb uses the me(n)- prefix. Note that, depending on the initial sound of the root word, the n of this prefix can take the form of ng, ny or m, or may not appear at all. Also, the root-word is sometimes modified. For instance, the root-word tulis, 'write' drops the t and becomes menulis 'to write'.

Root		Verb	
answer	jawab	to answer	menjawab
take	ambil	to take	mengambil
sing	anyi	to sing	menyanyi
read	baca	to read	membaca
feel	rasa	to feel	merasa

There are numerous other types of verbs which have prefixes and suffixes such as memper-, di-, -i and -kan. When learning these verb forms, you'll soon find that this is where many of Indonesian's irregularities lie. For example, the root-word kata, 'word', has the following mutations:

memperkatakan	to talk about ...
dikatakan	to be said
mengata-ngatai	to scold
mengatakan	to say that ...
berkata	to say

However, remember that in everyday speech, using the root-word alone within a sentence will still convey a clear meaning.

Tense

Thankfully, verbs don't change their form according to tense. Instead, tense can be expressed by using a word describing time – such as besok, 'tomorrow' or kemarin, 'yesterday' – at the beginning or end of a sentence.

Yesterday I bought a car.	Kemarin saya membeli mobil. (lit: yesterday I to-buy car)
Tomorrow I will buy a car.	Besok saya membeli mobil. (lit: tomorrow I to-buy car)

Alternatively, certain adverbs and auxiliaries may be used to indicate time in a sentence, immediately before the verb. The most common are:

already	sudah
currently	sedang
have just	baru
not yet	belum
still	masih
will	akan

I'm currently eating.	Saya sedang makan. (lit: I currently eat)
We already swam.	Kami sudah berenang. (lit: we already to-swim)

INDONESIANS SPEAKING ENGLISH

- When speaking English, Indonesians often have trouble with the letters 'f' and 'p', rendering sentences like 'Paul is packing for a picnic' potentially dangerous.
- Tenses can make for confusing sentences, as in 'Yesterday I will go home'.
- As separate pronouns for 'he' and 'she' don't exist in Indonesian, they're often liberally exchanged, as in 'She is my brother'.
- Distinctions between singular and plural are often overlooked or confused, as in the sentence 'I have many sister'.

ESSENTIAL VERBS

to be able	bisa
to become	menjadi
to bring	membawa
to buy	membeli
to come	datang
to cost	berharga
to depart/leave	berangkat
to drink	minum
to eat	makan
to give	memberi
to go	pergi
to have	punya
to know (someone)	kenal
to know (something)	tahu
to like	suka
to live (life)	hidup
to live (somewhere)	tinggal
to love	cinta
to make	membuat
to meet	bertemu
to need	perlu
to prefer	lebih suka
to return	kembali
to say	berkata
to stay (remain)	tetap
to stay (somewhere)	tinggal
to take	mengambil
to understand	mengerti
to want	mau

TO BE

There's no direct equivalent of 'to be' in Indonesian. No word is required when describing occupations or states of being.

I am a doctor.	Saya dokter. (lit: I doctor)
I'm hungry.	Saya lapar. (lit: I hungry)

To say that something does or doesn't exist, the word ada, 'there is/are' (lit: to-exist) can be used in a sentence which has no definite subject. (See page 36 for other uses of ada.)

Is there a night bus?	Ada bis malam? (lit: to-exist bus night?)

TO HAVE

The verb 'to have' has two variations in Indonesian. Ada is the most common and the most useful. Ada can be used to find out if something exists or is available, the same way that English speakers use the construction 'Do you have a ...?' or 'Is there a ...?'

Do you have a room?	Ada kamar? (lit: have room?)

Punya is more commonly used when talking about personal possession.

I have a child.	Saya punya anak. (lit: I have child)

IMPERATIVES

If you're asking, insisting or demanding that someone does something, no prefix is needed on the verb.

Wait!	Tunggu! (lit: wait!)

To make the command more polite, add silahkan 'please' before the verb.

Please sit down.	Silahkan duduk. (lit: please sit)

QUESTION WORDS

These question words can appear at either the beginning or the end of a sentence.

What?	**Apa?**	What does he like? **Dia suka apa?** (lit: he likes what?)
Who?/ Whose?	**Siapa?**	Who is she? **Siapa dia?** (lit: who she?)
When?	**Kapan?**	When does this bus leave? **Kapan bis ini berangkat?** (lit: when bus this leave?)
How?	**Bagaimana?**	What's this hotel like? **Bagaimana hotel ini?** (lit: how hotel this?)
Why?	**Mengapa?/ Kenapa?**	Why is the bus late? **Bisnya terlambat mengapa?** (lit: the-bus late why?)

There are three versions of the word 'where' in Indonesian.

At where?	**Mana?**	Where's the station? **Stasiun di mana?** (lit: station at where?)
From where?	**Dari mana?**	Where have you come from? **Anda datang dari mana?** (lit: you come from where?)
To where?	**Mana?**	Where does this bus go to? **Bis ini pergi ke mana?** (lit: bus this go to where?)

QUESTION WORDS

Questions that will be answered with a numeral always include the word berapa, 'how much/many'.

How much/ many?	Berapa?	How much is this? Berapa harga ini? (lit: how-much cost this?)

QUESTIONS

As with English, a question can be formed by simply raising the pitch of your voice at the end of a sentence.

Other ways to form questions include:

- starting a sentence with **apakah**, 'is it that ...?'

  Is the river cold? — **Apakah sungai ini dingin?** (lit: is-it-that river this cold?)

- adding **nggak**, 'no' to the end of a query

  Is it spicy or not? — **Pedas, nggak?** (lit: spicy, no?)

- with nouns, adding **'kan** (short for **bukan**, meaning 'not') to the end of the sentence

  This car, right? — **Mobil ini, 'kan?** (lit: car this, no?)

- adding a question word at the beginning or end of a sentence (see Question Words, pages 34-35)

Answers

Indonesians commonly answer questions concerning availability or possession with ada 'have' or tidak ada 'don't have'.

Is there a room free?	Apakah ada kamar kosong? (lit: is-it-that have room free?)
Yes.	Ada. (lit: have)
No.	Tidak ada. (lit: not have)

NO!

The word tidak, 'no', naturally pops up in speech all the time, although you often wouldn't recognise it. It's regularly shortened to tak, or somehow pronounced as a gurgling ngggaaaak

With questions to do with status or experience, such as 'Are you married?' or 'Have you been to Iceland?', the common answer is either sudah, 'already' or belum, 'not yet'. Answering ya, 'yes' or tidak, 'no' is not incorrect, but suggests that you won't ever marry, or go to Iceland.

Whether you intend to do these things or not, using sudah/belum is the more optimistic response.

Are you married?	Sudah kawin? (lit: already married?)
Yes./No.	Sudah./Belum. (lit: already/not-yet)

NEGATIVES

Three words in Indonesian are used to express the negative. These are tidak 'no', bukan 'not' and jangan 'don't'.

Bukan is used in relation to nouns.

Not that car.	Bukan mobil itu. (lit: not car that)

Both tidak and jangan are used in relation to verbs and adjectives.

I don't want to.	Saya tidak mau. (lit: I no want)
Do not enter.	Jangan masuk. (lit: don't enter)

PREPOSITIONS

Prepositions are used the same way as in English.

about (concerns)	tentang/mengenai
at (place)	di
at (time)	pada jam
between	di antara
during	selama
for	untuk
for (time)	selama
from	dari
in	dalam
in (place)	di
inside	di dalam
on (time/person)	pada
on (place)	di
since	sejak
through	melalui
to	ke
until	sampai
via	melalui
with	dengan
without	tanpa

This story is about war.	Cerita ini mengenai perang. (lit: story this concerns war)
We'll meet at 3pm.	Kita bertemu pada jam tiga. (lit: we to-meet at hour three)
From Sabang to Merauke.	Dari Sabang ke Merauke. (lit: from Sabang to Merauke)
I'm not fluent in Indonesian yet.	Saya belum lancar dalam Bahasa Indonesia. (lit: I not-yet fluent in language-of Indonesia)

CONJUNCTIONS

after	sesudah
because	karena/sebab
before	sebelum
if	kalau
or	atau
since	sejak
when	waktu
while	sedang/sementara

We've been sleeping since 2 o'clock.	Kami tidur sejak jam dua. (lit: we to-sleep since hour two)
This cake or that cake?	Kue ini atau kue itu? (lit: cake this or cake that?)

PERKENALAN

MEETING PEOPLE

Perhaps this chapter should be called 'being met', as Indonesians are quick to take the social initiative. First conversations tend to revolve around family, nationality, and your tolerance to spicy food.

The attention you receive can be exhausting, especially after a trans-Sumatran bus journey, so keep your cool and try asking questions instead of only answering them. Remember that the 14th person to ask ke mana, 'where are you going?' may think they are the first.

YOU SHOULD KNOW — ANDA PERLU TAHU

Hello.	Salam.
Goodbye.	Sampai jumpa.
Yes.	Ya.
No.	Tidak.
Excuse me.	Permisi.

There are two words for 'please' in Indonesian. Tolong, 'help', is used when you're making a request or asking somebody to do something for you.

Please. (when asking for something)	Tolong.
Please open the window.	Tolong buka jendela.

If you're offering something to somebody, use the word silahkan (lit: be-my-guest).

Please. (when offering something)	Silahkan.
Please sit down.	Silahkan duduk.

Thank you (very much).	Terima kasih (banyak).
You're welcome.	Kembali; Sama-sama.
Excuse me; Sorry.	Permisi.
May I?; Do you mind?	Boleh?
That's fine; No problem.	Boleh; Tidak apa-apa.
What did you say?	Tolong ulangi?
I'm sorry. (apology)	Ma'af.

THANKS, NO THANKS

Although the direct meaning of terima kasih, 'thank you', is straightforward, its implied meaning can be confusing. If you're offered something – a drink or some food – and you accept with terima kasih, you'll probably go hungry, as Indonesians use terima kasih as a polite term of refusal.

To accept an offer, say ya, 'yes', or boleh (lit: may). Apart from being used to refuse an offer, terima kasih is used as you would expect – to show appreciation.

GREETINGS & GOODBYES — UCAPAN SELAMAT

Indonesian greetings can range from a passing holler to a lengthy and formulaic exchange. Age, marital status, religion, time and situation can all play a part in what is said. Thankfully, across-the-board greetings exist which involve no risk of insult or of being inappropriate.

As an outsider, any attempt to use Indonesian will be well received, and since chatting to a stranger at a warung, 'street stall', is considered normal, you'll have plenty of opportunity to practise.

As in English, Indonesian greetings are based on the time of day. However, greetings don't change only in relation to the clock, but by things such as weather and routine – while you may think the day's just begun, the person you're speaking to may have already been to market and prepared lunch.

Good morning. (sunrise – 10 am) Selamat pagi.
the best time to be out and about, watching starched-uniformed children heading to school, people carrying produce to market, or taksi, 'taxi' drivers digging into a bowl of bubur ayam, 'chicken porridge'

Good day. (10 am – 4 pm) Selamat siang.
by this time the heat really has kicked in, as has the traffic

Good afternoon. (4 – sunset) Selamat sore.
the sun is beyond the danger zone and children's kites are filling the sky, or the punctual tropical downpour has begun

Good evening. (after dark) Selamat malam.
the pasar malam, 'night markets', are in full swing

Good night. (on retiring) Selamat tidur.

More informal greetings used between peers and friends include:

Hello.	Halo; Salam. (lit: peace)
Where are you going?	Ke mana? This is an ice breaker. Answering 'to the shops, then I'm off to Borobudur', would be overkill. The response jalan-jalan, 'travelling around', is sufficient.
How are things?	Gimana? Depending on context, Gimana? can also mean 'What did you say?'.

The word selamat comes from the Arabic word *salam*, meaning 'peace'. Putting this word together with 'morning' or 'evening' means something like 'Have a nice morning/evening'.

In Muslim areas of the country, you'll hear people use the Arabic greeting:

assalamualaikum	'peace be on you'

to which the response is:

alaikumsalam	'on you be peace'

Goodbyes — Selamat Tinggal

Farewell. (when you're leaving)	Selamat tinggal.
Farewell. (when others are leaving)	Selamat jalan.
Goodnight.	Selamat malam.
See you later.	Sampai jumpa.
I'm going home now.	Saya pulang dulu. (lit: I go-home now)
Bye.	Daag.

THEY MAY SAY ...

Selamat datang.	Welcome.
Silahkan masuk.	Please come in.
Selamat ...	Enjoy your ...
... dulu.	
makan	meal
minum	drink

FORMS OF ADDRESS — SAPAAN

It's a good idea to use 'sir' or 'ma'am' when talking directly to someone older or in a position of respect (these terms are the same as those for 'father' and 'mother').

sir	Pak (short for bapak)
ma'am	Bu (short for ibu)
Mr	Pak
Ms	Ibu
Mrs	Ibu
Miss (used for a female younger than you)	Mbak

FIRST ENCOUNTERS — PERTEMUAN PERTAMA

What's your name?	Siapa nama Anda?
My name's ...	Nama saya ...
I'd like to introduce you to ...	Kenalkan, nama dia ...
I'm pleased to meet you.	Saya senang bertemu dengan Anda.

WHO ARE YOU?

There are several forms of the pronoun 'you' that range in level of politeness:

(ka)mu (eng)kau	informal. Mu and kau are the shortened forms.
Anda	polite
saudara	respectful

When talking to someone of the same age or older, or to someone you want to show respect, the safest form of 'you' is one of the following:

bapak	sir
ibu	ma'am

MAKING CONVERSATION — PERCAKAPAN

Greetings aside, many people will launch straight into the guts of a conversation. Common starters include:

How are you?	Apa kabar?
Fine. And you?	Kabar baik. Apa kabar?
Where are you going?	Ke mana?

BREAKING THE ICE

Do you live here?	Apakah Anda tinggal di sini?
What are you doing?	Anda buat apa?
What do you think about ...?	Anda pikir apa tentang ...?
Beautiful, isn't it!	Indah, bukan!
It's very nice here.	Indah sekali di sini.
We love it here.	Kami senang di sini.
What a cute baby!	Bayinya lucu!
Are you waiting too?	Apakah Anda menunggu juga?
That's strange!	Aneh itu!
That's funny! (amusing)	Lucu itu!

Remember that the phrase ke mana?, 'where are you going?' is simply a conversation starter. Easy answers to ke mana? include:

To (Denpasar).	Ke (Denpasar).
Travelling/Sightseeing.	Jalan-jalan.
Out and about.	Makan angin. (lit: eating the breeze)

One of the first things people will want to know about you is where you're from and why you're in Indonesia.

How long have you been in Indonesia?	Sudah berapa lama di Indonesia?
I've been here for two weeks.	Saya sudah dua minggu di Indonesia.
How long do you plan to stay in Indonesia?	Rencananya berapa lama Anda di Indonesia?
I plan to be here for (one month).	Rencana saya (satu bulan) di Indonesia.
Where have you been so far?	Sudah ke mana?
I've been to Jakarta and Bandung.	Saya sudah ke Jakarta dan Bandung.
Have you been to Bali?	Sudah ke Bali?
Not yet.	Belum.
Yes I have.	Sudah.
Are you here on holiday?	Apakah Anda sedang libur?
I'm here ...	Saya ...
for a holiday	berlibur
on business	bekerja/berbisnis
to study	belajar

THEY MAY SAY ...

Indonesians can be very complimentary, and very honest.

Anda cantik.	You're beautiful.
Anda ganteng.	You're handsome.
Anda pandai.	You're clever.
Rambut anda cantik.	Your hair is beautiful.
Anda gemuk/kurus.	You're fat/skinny.
So are you.	Anda juga.

How long are you here for?	Berapa lama Anda di sini?
I'm/We're here for ... weeks/days.	Saya/Kami di sini selama ... minggu/hari.
Do you like it here?	Apakah anda senang di sini?
I/We like it here very much.	Saya/Kami senang sekali di sini.
It's very interesting here.	Menarik sekali di sini.
Can you eat spicy food?	Bisa makan makanan pedas?
I like spicy food.	Saya suka makanan pedas.

USEFUL PHRASES — ISTILAH YANG BERGUNA

Sure.	Betul.
Just a minute.	Sebentar.
It's OK.	Tidak apa apa.
Are you ready?	Siap?
Good luck!	Selamat!
Wait!	Tunggu!
Look!	Lihat!
Listen!	Dengarlah!
I'm ready.	Saya siap.
Slow down!	Pelan-pelan!
Hurry up!	Cepat-cepat!
Go away!	Pergi!
Watch out!	Awas!
It's (not) possible.	(Tidak) boleh.
I forgot.	Saya lupa.
It's (not) important.	(Tidak) penting.
Do you live here?	Anda tinggal di sini?
It doesn't matter.	Tidak apa-apa.

NATIONALITIES KEBANGSAAN

You'll find that many country names in Indonesian are similar to English. Remember though, even if a word looks like the English equivalent, it will have a Indonesian pronunciation. If you still can't explain, try pointing to the map.

WHERE ARE YOU COMING FROM?

If you want to ask someone where they're from, you should specify if you mean just now, or originally.

Where have you just come from?	Anda dari mana?
Where are you originally from?	Anda berasal dari mana?
Where do you live?	Anda tinggal di mana?
Where do your parents live?	Orang-tuanya tinggal di mana?

Where are you from?	Anda berasal dari mana?
I'm from ...	Saya berasal dari ...
Australia	Australia
Canada	Kanada
England	Inggris
Europe	Eropa
India	India
Ireland	Irlandia
Japan	Jepang
New Zealand	Selandia Baru
Scotland	Skotlandia
the USA	Amerika
Wales	Wales

I'm ...	Saya orang ...
Australian	Australia
American	Amerika
British	Inggris
Canadian	Kanada
Dutch	Belanda
English	Inggris
Irish	Irlandia
New Zealander	Selandia Baru
Welsh	Wales

I live in a/the ...	Saya tinggal di ...
city	kota
countryside	luar kota
mountains	pegunungan
seaside	pantai
suburbs of ...	bagian pinggir kota ...
village	kampung

CAN YOU BE LUCU?

The word lucu can mean either 'funny' (humorous) or 'cute' (as in a baby). So if you're able to read this then your chances of being both at the same time are minimal.

CULTURAL DIFFERENCES — PERBEDAAN KEBUDAYAAN

How do you do this in your country?	Bagaimana ini dibuat di negara anda?
Is this a local or national custom?	Adat ini adat daerah atau adat nasional?
I don't want to offend you.	Saya tidak mau menyinggung perasaan Anda.

I'm sorry, it's not the custom in my country. — Ma'af, adat ini tidak biasa di negara saya.

I'm not accustomed to this. — Ini tidak biasa untuk saya

I don't mind watching, but I'd prefer not to participate. — Saya lebih senang menonton daripada mengikuti aktivitasnya.

AGE — UMUR

Age isn't a sensitive issue in Indonesia, so expect to be asked yours often. Ask people to guess by saying coba terka.

How old are you? — Berapa umur Anda?

How old is your child? — Berapa umur anaknya?

I'm ... years old. — Umur saya ... tahun.

20 — dua-puluh

35 — tiga-puluh lima

(See Numbers & Amounts on page 187 for your age.)

BAGUS

Visitors often like using the word bagus, meaning 'great'. But remember that a person can't be bagus. Instead they can be baik hati, 'good hearted', murah hati, 'generous' or simply baik, 'good' – but not bagus.

OCCUPATIONS — PEKERJAAN

What's your occupation?	Apa pekerjaan Anda?
What do you do?	Anda bekerja sebagai apa?
I'm (a/an) ...	Saya ...
artist	seniman
businessperson	pengusaha
chef	pemasak
doctor	dokter
engineer	insinyur
factory worker	pekerja pabrik
farmer	petani
journalist	wartawan
lawyer	ahli hukum
lecturer (university)	dosen
mechanic	montir
musician	pemain musik
nurse	perawat
office worker	pegawai
public servant	pegawai negeri
retired	pensiunan
sailor	pelaut
singer	penyanyi
scientist	ilmuwan
secretary	sekretaris
student (school)	pelajar
student (university)	mahasiswa
teacher (school)	guru
unemployed	penganggur
waiter	pelayan
writer	penulis

PUTTING YOUR FOOT IN IT

When visiting someone's home, it's customary to take your shoes off at the door. If visiting a mesjid, 'mosque', it's obligatory to take your shoes off.

What are you studying? Anda belajar apa?

I'm studying ... Saya belajar ...

art	kesenian
arts/humanities	ilmu sastera
business	bisnis
engineering	keahlian teknik
languages	bahasa-bahasa
law	hukum
medicine	ilmu kedokteran
Indonesian	bahasa Indonesia
science	ilmu sains
teaching	pengajaran

SAYING NO

It's not appropriate.	Ini tidak cocok.
I'm busy.	Saya sibuk.
I don't have time.	Saya tidak ada waktu.

RELIGION AGAMA

What's your religion? Anda beragama apa?

My religion is ... Agama saya ...

Buddhist	Buda
Catholic	Katolik
Christian	Kristen
Hindu	Hindu
Jewish	Yahudi
Muslim	Islam
Protestant	Protestan

Most Indonesians are Muslim, and many others are Christian, Hindu or Buddhist. Indonesians may feel uncomfortable if you don't profess a religion, as religion's a major part of the nation's ideology (see boxed text on page 93).

You'll maintain better relations by claiming to have a religion, or to say your parents belong to a religion.

I'm not religious.	Saya tidak beragama.
I'm (Catholic), but not practising.	Saya beragama (Katolik) tapi jarang ke gereja.
My parents are (Catholic).	Orang tua saya beragama (Katolik).
I think I believe in God.	Saya kira saya percaya kepada Tuhan.
I believe in destiny/fate.	Saya percaya kepada nasib.
I'm interested in astrology/ philosophy.	Saya tertarik pada astrologi/ filsafat.
I'm an atheist.	Saya atheis.
I'm agnostic.	Saya agnostik.

BOLEH?

Two useful words to know when making a request or asking permission are boleh, 'May I?' (lit: possible) and minta, which loosely translates as 'could you please'.

May I come in?	Boleh saya masuk? (lit: possible I enter?)
Could you please give me a pen?	Bisa kasih pena? (lit: can give pen?)

BODY LANGUAGE BAHASA TUBUH

• Handshaking is accepted between both sexes right across Indonesia, but a gentle squeeze as opposed to a knuckle-crushing grip is the way to go. To add warmth and sincerity, you'll find that many people follow the handshake with a touch of the heart, a habit worth forming.

It's appropriate to shake hands when being introduced to somebody, when visiting somebody in their home, or when you haven't seen someone for a while. When meeting somebody for the first time, Indonesians often shake hands while telling you their name.

• In cases which warrant extreme respect, such as when a young child greets an elder, the child will kiss the elder's hand then touch it to their own forehead.

In some areas, especially in Java, you'll see people greet each other by pressing their palms together, with the right hand slightly forward, and lightly touching the fingertips of other person's right hand.

• Left-handedness in Indonesia is considered an anomaly, and children are coerced into using their right hand from an early age. This is because Indonesians use the left hand for cleaning themselves.

It's a good idea to get into the habit of using your right hand for passing items and even eating. If you're left handed, you'll probably be called kidal, 'lefty'.

• It's considered polite to bow your body slightly when crossing the path of someone who's seated, or when interrupting people. At the same time you can say permisi, 'excuse me'.

• Apart from shaking hands, physical contact between the sexes is very minimal in Indonesian society. However, contact between the same sex is considered normal behaviour, and not at all sexual. You'll see boys hanging out with their arms around each other's shoulders, and women can be very affectionate to their close friends. If you have pale skin or long blonde hair, there'll be someone who wants to know what it feels like.

• It's been said that touching someone's head is considered rude. This may be the case with an older person, but you'll see people of the same age touching their friend's hair and people patting children on the head all the time.

• To many Indonesians, westerners come across as a hurried lot. Indeed, Indonesians seem to take things at a slower pace – and considering the climate, crowds, and the effort needed to get around – slowing down is probably a healthy option.

PROKEM – JAKARTA SLANG

Originating on the streets of Jakarta as a hybrid of the Indonesian and Javanese languages and of Betawi, the regional language of Jakarta, Prokem, was shunned as the low-class jargon of Jakarta's urban youth. Despite this, the influence of Prokem has travelled from the streets of the capital to markets and towns as far away as Kupang.

These days there are Prokem dictionaries, and you'll hear people of all ages interspersing everyday Indonesian with Prokem phrases. To the untrained ear, Prokem can sound like gutteral gunfire.

Some common Prokem words you might hear are:

Prokem	Indonesian	
boil	mobil	car
bokap	bapak	father/sir
doski	dia	s/he
ember	bohong	to lie
geblek	goblok	stupid
gesek plastic	pakai kartu kredit	paying with credit card
jaing	anjing	dog
nyimeng/ ngeboat	makan obat terlarang	to take drugs (narcotics)
nyokap	ibu	mother/ma'am
rokun	rumah	house

FEELINGS / PERASAAN

I'm ...	Saya ...
Are you ...?	Apakah Anda ...?
afraid	takut
angry	marah
bored	bosan
cold	dingin
full	kenyang
grateful	berterima kasih
happy	senang
hot	panas
hungry	lapar
in a hurry	tergesa-gesa
keen	ingin sekali
right (contented)	puas
sad	sedih
scared	takut
sick	sakit
sleepy	ngantuk
sorry (condolence)	merasa kasihan
sorry (regret)	menyesal
thirsty	haus
tired	lelah/letih
well	baik
worried	kawatir

PE!

Adding the prefix pe- to a root word often results in the creation of a noun for a person's occupation.

Root Word		Noun	
paint	lumkis	painter	pelukis
run	lari	runner	pelari

HOME TRUTHS

Many Indonesians are quick to offer an invitation to their home, and it's customary to swap addresses or business cards. An Indonesian's home is where formalities really kick in, and the informality you may have experienced on the street will often be replaced with an almost uncomfortable reverence.

As a guest, you'll be expected to do absolutely nothing while your hosts prepare refreshments and shoo away peering children. Since any attempt to help with preparing food or cleaning up will almost certainly be met with cries of **jangan repot**, 'don't trouble yourself', it's best to let things happen around you. Bringing along photos and maps is a great way to encourage your host to relax.

If there are older people in the room, it's polite to approach and greet them with your head slightly bowed.

For many Indonesians, it's a sign of polite restraint not to accept an offer when it's first made. Therefore, if you're offering something, don't be deterred by a first refusal. Repeat the offer, and it will probably be accepted.

When you're visiting somebody in their home, you may be served tea, coffee or a sweet drink, as well as biscuits or other snacks. It's customary to wait until these are offered before eating. If something's not to your liking, it's quite acceptable to take just a few sips. If you don't want to take the snack, just say:

Ma'af, saya baru makan. Sorry, I've just eaten.

Delicious!	Enak.
I should go home now.	Permisi, pulang dulu.
Thanks for your hospitality.	Terima kasih atas keramah-tamahannya.

BREAKING THE LANGUAGE BARRIER / MENGATASI KESUKARAN BAHASA

Do you speak English?	Apakah Anda berbahasa Inggris?
Yes./No.	Ya./Tidak bisa.
I can only speak a little Indonesian.	Saya hanya berbahasa Indonesia sedikit saja.
Does any one here speak English?	Ada orang yang berbahasa Inggris di sini?
Do you understand?	Apakah Anda mengerti?
I (don't) understand.	Saya (tidak) mengerti.

How do you say ... in Indonesian?	Apa bahasa Indonesianya ...?
What's this called?	Apa ini?
What does this mean?	Apa artinya ini?
Please speak slowly!	Tolong bicara lebih pelan.
Please write that word down for me.	Tolong tuliskan kata itu untuk saya.
Please repeat that.	Tolong ulangi.
Please translate for me.	Tolong terjemahkan untuk saya.

STAYING IN TOUCH — MEMBUAT JANJI

Where are you staying?	Anda menginap di mana?
What's your address?	Alamat Anda apa?
I'm staying at ...	Saya menginap di ...
Can we meet again?	Apakah kita bertemu lagi?
When should we meet?	Jam berapa kita bertemu?
Let's meet at (6 o'clock) in the square.	Kita bertemu (jam enam) di alun-alun.
Come and visit any time.	Kapan saja main di rumah saya.

JALAN-JALAN — GETTING AROUND

Travelling in Indonesia requires both patience and flexibility. Trains slow down for no apparent reason, roads disappear in torrents of rain, and flight schedules change without notice. Nevertheless, as long as there are passengers, you will make it to your destination.

FINDING YOUR WAY — ORIENTASI

Excuse me.	Permisi.
I'm lost.	Saya tersesat.
Where's the ...?	... di mana?
airport	Lapangan terbang; Bandar udara; Bandara
(inter)city bus station	Terminal bis (antar) kota
road to (Solo)	Jalan ke (Solo)
train station	Stasiun kereta api

INI DAN ITU

Instead of using the definite article 'the', Indonesian makes more use of the words ini 'this' and itu 'that' when speaking of a specific object.

that red hat	topi merah itu (lit: hat red that)

What time does the ... leave/arrive?	... berangkat/tiba jam berapa?
(inter)city bus	Bis (antar) kota
plane	Pesawat udara/terbang
ship	Kapal
train	Kereta api
How can I get to ...?	Saya bisa naik apa ke ...?
Is it near/far?	Apakah dekat/jauh?
Can we walk there?	Bisa jalan kaki ke sana?
Can you show me (on the map)?	Tolong tunjukkan (di peta).
Are there other means of getting there?	Ada cara perjalanan lain?
What street is this?	Jalan ini jalan apa?
What ... is this?	... ini ... apa?
city	kota
village	desa/kampung

UP THE JUNCTION

What a road junction is called in Indonesia depends upon how many roads converge on it. A three-road junction – a T-junction – is known as a pertigaan and a four-road junction, or crossroad, is a perempatan. Good thing there aren't any persembilanbelasan, '19-road junctions'.

DIRECTIONS — PETUNJUK

(Go) straight ahead!	(Jalan) terus!
To the left/right.	Ke kiri/kanan.
Turn left/right at the ...	Belok kiri/kanan di ...
corner	sudut/pojok
intersection	perempatan
next corner	sudut yang berikutnya
T-junction	pertigaan
traffic lights	lampu merah

in front of	di depan/di muka
next to	di samping
behind	di belakang
opposite	berlawanan
near	dekat
far	jauh

north	utara
south	selatan
east	timur
west	barat
north-east	(utara) timur laut
north-west	(utara) barat laut
south-east	tenggara
south-west	barat daya

GOING THE DISTANCE

Knowing how far away a place is doesn't always bear a relation to how long it's going to take to get there. Travelling 20km on a rough road can take as long as 100km on a jalan tol, 'toll road'.

How long (time/distance) is the journey?	Berapa lama/jauh perjalanannya?
It's 50km away.	Jaraknya lima-puluh kilometer.
The trip takes two hours.	Lamanya dua jam.
distance	jarak
length of time	lama

ADDRESSES **ALAMAT**

Indonesian city addresses look similar to this:

> Elang Maliharja
> Jl. Banda 23
> RT 08 RW 10
> Ciumbuleuit
> Bandung 40142
> Jabar

This means Elang Maliharja lives in:

- Banda Street (**Jalan**) number 23
- Neighbourhood (**Rukun Tetangga**) number 8, Ciumbuleuit
- Administrative Unit (**Rukun Warga**) number 10, Bandung (Administrative units are made up of several neighbourhoods.)
- the province of West Java, (**Jabar**, short for **Jawa Barat**)

Other abbreviated province names include **Jatim** (**Jawa Timur**) and **NTT** (**Nusa Tenggara Timur**).

Outside main cities, addresses may include the following:

> Asti Basteui
> Jl. Perkedel 3
> Kampung Mangga, Desa Nyamuk
> Kec. Gorengan, Kab. Lele
> Jabar

Kampung means village, **Desa** means village area, **Kecamatan** (**Kec.**) means subdistrict and **Kabupaten** (**Kab.**) means regency.

BUYING TICKETS — MEMBELI KARCIS

Ticket prices are usually posted for ferry, night bus and train travel. For shorter distance transport, ask other passengers. You may have to bargain for a fare reduction (see Bargaining on page 121). On day buses, tickets are usually sold during the journey from the kenek (see boxed text on page 66).

How much does it cost to go to ...?	Berapa ongkosnya ke ...?
How much is it from Jakarta to Medan?	Berapa ongkosnya dari Jakarta ke Medan?
Where can I buy a ticket?	Tiket dijual di mana?
We want to go to ...	Kami mau ke ...
Do I need to book?	Apakah harus pesan?
I'd like to book a seat to ...	Saya mau memesan tempat duduk ke ...
I'd like (a) ...	Saya mau ...
one-way ticket	tiket satu jalan
return ticket	tiket pulang pergi
two tickets	dua tiket
student's fare	harga mahasiswa
child's/pensioner's fare	harga anak/pensiun
1st class	kelas satu/eksekutif
2nd class	kelas dua/bisnis
economy class	kelas ekonomi

BARGAINING

That's too much!	Terlalu mahal!
What's the normal fare?	Harga biasa berapa?
How about Rp 500?	Bagaimana kalau lima-ratus rupiah?
Here's Rp1000.	Ini uangnya seribu rupiah.

How about my change?	Mana kembalinya?
confirmation	kepastian/konfirmasi
destination	tempat tujuan
reservation office	kantor pemesanan
timetable	daftar waktu/jadwal
ticket	karcis/tiket
ticket window	loket
seat	tempat duduk; kursi
station (master)	(kepala) stasiun

AIR — PESAWAT UDARA

Is there a flight to Medan on (Monday)?	Apakah ada pesawat ke Medan pada (hari Senin)?
What time is the flight to Medan on (Monday)?	Jam berapa pesawat berangkat ke Medan pada (hari Senin)?
What time do I have to be at the airport?	Jam berapa saya harus ada di bandara?
When's the next flight to (Cebu)?	Kapan pesawat berikut ke (Cebu)?
I'd like to reconfirm my ticket to Medan.	Saya mau memastikan tiket saya ke Medan.
How long does the flight take?	Perjalanannya berapa lama?
Where's the baggage claim?	Pengambilan barang di mana?

SIGNS

BARANG HILANG	LOST PROPERTY
KEBERANGKATAN	DEPARTURES
KEDATANGAN	ARRIVALS
MENDAFTARKAN DIRI	CHECK-IN
PENGAWASAN PASPOR	PASSPORT CONTROL

Customs — Pabean; Bea dan Cukai

I have nothing to declare.	Barang saya tidak perlu dilaporkan.
I have something to declare.	Ada barang saya yang perlu dilaporkan.
Do I have to declare this?	Apakah ini harus dilaporkan?
This is all my luggage.	Ini semua barang saya.
I didn't know I had to declare it.	Saya tidak tahu barang ini harus dilaporkan.
aeroplane	pesawat udara/terbang
airport	lapangan terbang; bandar udara; bandara
landing	pendaratan
steward (m/f)	pramugara/pramugari

BUS — BIS

The quickest way to travel long distances is to take an express bus. These buses make occasional meal and toilet stops and can only be boarded at city terminals. Buses range from the spartan to the deluxe, and you pay accordingly. However, you miss the day-to-day roadside activity, especially if travelling by night.

BUS'N A MOVE

There's a great variety of local transport in Indonesia, including the ubiquitous Balinese bemo, or minibus. In some towns, bemos are known as angkot, from angkutan, 'transport' and kota, 'city'.

A step up from the bemo is the small minibus known either as oplet; mikrolet; angkudes (from angkutan, 'transport' and desa, 'village'); or kolt, after Mitsubishi Colt. These minibuses often run between villages or nearby towns. Prices vary but are always cheap. Some places have a flat rate; in others, price depends on the distance.

Non-express buses are slower, as they can be hailed anywhere along the road. Long-distance travel on bumpy roads can be tedious, uncomfortable and crowded, so if it's possible, sit in the middle of the bus. Avoid sitting next to the driver, as gear changes may ruin your kneecaps and overtaking techniques may leave you a nervous wreck.

An alternative to large buses are **travel** – small buses or minivans that carry about 12 people and offer pick-up and drop-off services. Although this is a convenient service, picking up and dropping off 12 people across a large town can take a long time.

Which bus goes to ...?	**Bis yang mana ke ...?**
Does this bus go to ...?	**Apakah bis ini ke ...?**
Do buses come often?	**Apakah bis sering lewat?**
Often/Rarely.	**Sering/Jarang.**
Where do I get the bus for ...?	**Bis ke ... di mana?**

ALL HAIL THE BUS

An essential part of every bus or **bemo** is the **kenek**, 'assistant' (from the Dutch word for 'boy', *knecht*).

The job of the **kenek** is to tout for passengers, collect fares and help squeeze in the load. You'll easily recognise the **kenek**, as he'll be the one swinging from the door of the bus asking every pedestrian if they have a sudden urge to go to Lampung. They repeatedly call out the destination until the name turns into a meditative chant:

Jojajojajojajojajojajojajojajojaaaa!
Would you like to go to Yogyakarta?

Sobosobosobosobosobosobosobosoboooo!
A trip to Wonosobo, perhaps?

Lwitlwitlwitlwitlwitlwitlwitlwiiiit!
Yes indeed, we're heading to Ciumbuleuit!

What time's the ... bus (to ...)?	Jam berapa bis ... (ke ...)?
first	pertama
last	terakhir
next	berikutnya
Will the bus stop at a restaurant?	Apakah bisnya berhenti di restoran?
Could you let me know when we arrive at ...	Tolong beritahu saya kalau sudah sampai di ...
Where are we now?	Kita sedang di mana?
I want to get off!	Kiri (depan)!; Stop!

STOOD UP

The (train) is ...	(Kereta)nya ...
cancelled	dibatalkan
delayed (intentional)	ditunda
delayed (unexpected)	tertunda
late	terlambat
on time	tepat
How long will it be delayed?	Berapa lama ditundanya/tertundanya?

TRAIN — KERETA

Train travel is only available in Java and South Sumatra. It's a good alternative for the bus-weary traveller, and there's a wide choice as far as comfort and speed are concerned, with corresponding prices. For longer trips, you'll need to book a seat. Purchase your ticket before boarding, or in advance during Lebaran and other holidays.

I want to go by express train to ...	Saya mau naik kereta ekspres ke ...
Which platform does the train leave from?	Dari peron berapa keretanya berangkat?

Where do I need to change trains?	Saya ganti kereta di mana?
Does this train stop at Naga?	Apakah kereta ini berhenti di Naga?
Can I get off at Naga?	Apakah saya bisa turun di Naga?
Is this seat free?	Apakah kursi ini kosong?
This seat's taken.	Sudah ada orang.
Would you mind if I open the window?	Boleh saya buka jendela?
What's ... station?	Apa namanya stasiun ...?
this	ini
the next	yang berikutnya
Do I need to change trains?	Apakah saya harus ganti kereta?
You must change at ...	Anda harus ganti di ...
I want to get off at ...	Saya mau turun di ...

TAXI — TAKSI

There are both official and unofficial taxis in Indonesia. Official taxis always have a sign and usually an argo, 'meter'. In unofficial taxis, you'll have to agree on a price before setting out.

Taxis without meters are usually hired hourly or daily. Often the driver of an official taxi would rather set a fixed price than use the meter. If you know how much the trip should cost, you can bargain for a reasonable fare, otherwise insist on using the meter.

WHERES A CAB WHEN YOU NEED ONE?

Need to catch a taxi, becak, 'rickshaw' or bajaj, '3-wheeled taxi'? Or just want to attract attention to yourself? Just clap your hands. Clapping to attract attention may seem rude, but it's what fare-hunting drivers listen out for.

Is this taxi available?	Apakah taksinya kosong?
Please use the meter.	Pakai argo saja.
How much is the fare?	Berapa ongkosnya?
Please take me to ...	Tolong antar saya ke ...
this address	alamat ini
the airport	bandara

SICK OF TRAVEL?

I feel nauseous.	Saya mual.
I'm going to vomit.	Saya mau muntah.
Is the road ...?	Apakah jalannya ...?
hilly	berbukit-bukit
windy	berbelok-belok
The driver's crazy!	Sopirnya gila!
I don't want to die!	Saya tidak mau meninggal!
(massive) traffic jam	macet (terus)

Instructions — Perintah

Here's fine, thanks.	Berhenti di sini saja.
The next street, please.	Jalan berikutnya.
The next street (to the left/right).	Jalan berikutnya (di sebelah kiri/kanan).
Continue!	Terus!
Please slow down.	Pelan-pelan saja.
Please hurry.	Tolong cepat sedikit.
Stop here!	Kiri!/Stop!
Stop at the corner.	Kiri di sudut.
Please wait here.	Tolong tunggu di sini.
I'll be right back.	Saya segera kembali.

THEY MAY SAY ...

Sudah penuh.	It's full.
Tidak ada kursi lagi.	There aren't any seats.
Tidak usah pesan.	There's no need to book.
Tempatnya tidak bisa dipesan.	You can't book a seat.
Tempatnya ada besok.	There are seats for tomorrow.

BOAT — KAPAL

Boat travel varies incredibly throughout the archipelago, from massive passenger ships to trans-river bathtubs.

boat	perahu
cabin	ruang
dock	dok
harbour	pelabuhan/bandar
port	bandar/pelabuhan
river	sungai/kali
sail	layar
sea	laut
ship	kapal

Where does the boat leave from?	Kapalnya berangkat di mana?
What time does the boat arrive at ...?	Jam berapa kapalnya tiba di ...?

CAR — MOBIL

Car hire is possible throughout Indonesia, if not through a company then through private arrangement. Usually a sopir, 'driver', can be organised, which isn't a bad idea since traffic laws often verge on the anarchic.

SIGNS

BERI JALAN	GIVE WAY
DILARANG ...	NO ...
MASUK	ENTRY
PARKIR	PARKING
JALAN TOL	TOLLWAY
PERBAIKAN JALAN	ROADWORKS
SATU ARAH	ONE WAY
TEMPAT PARKIR	CAR PARK

Where can I hire a car?	Saya bisa menyewa mobil di mana?
How much is it daily/weekly?	Berapa ongkos sewanya sehari/seminggu?
Does that include insurance?	Apakah ongkosnya termasuk asuransi?
Can we get a driver?	Bisa dapat sopir?
Where's the next petrol station?	Pompa bensin yang berikutnya di mana?
I want ... litres of petrol.	Minta ... liter bensin.
Please fill up the tank.	Tolong isi sampai penuh.

MAGIC MECHANICS

An alternative to taking your car to the bengkel, or 'garage/mechanic' is to take it to a ketok magic (lit: magic knocker). These garages are easily recognisable as they are completely enclosed. This is so the curious cannot see the how the montir, 'mechanic' works. The believers say they use magic – the skeptics say they use tools like any other mechanic.

Please check the ...	Tolong periksa ...
oil	oli
tyre pressure	tekanan ban
water	air
Is this the road to ...?	Apakah jalan ini jalan ke ...?
Can I park here?	Bisa parkir di sini?
How much does it cost to park here?	Berapa biaya parkir di sini?

air	udara
battery	aki/baterai
brakes	rem
car	mobil
clutch	kopeling
driver	sopir
drivers licence	SIM (Surat Izin Mengemudi) (lit: form permission to-drive)
engine	mesin
garage	garasi
horn	klakson
indicator	penunjuk/lampu sen
lights	lampu
main road	jalan raya/utama
oil	oli
petrol (gas)	bensin
diesel	solar
premium unleaded	premix
unleaded	premium
puncture	kebocoran/pecah
radiator	radiator
roadmap	peta jalan
seatbelt (rare)	sabuk pengaman
self-service (rare)	pelayanan sendiri
speed limit (rare)	batas kecepatan
tyres	ban
windscreen	kaca depan

DID YOU KNOW ...

If lined bumper to bumper, it's said the length of cars in Indonesia would be greater than the length of road available.

Car Problems / Masalah Mobil

We need a mechanic.	Kami mencari montir.
What make is it?	Merek apa mobilnya?
The car broke down at ...	Mobilnya mogok di ...
The car isn't working.	Mobilnya mogok.
The engine's dead.	Mesinnya mati.
It's overheating.	Mesinnya terlalu panas.
I've run out of petrol.	Bensinnya habis.
The battery's flat.	Baterainya habis.
The radiator's leaking.	Radiatornya bocor.
I have a flat tyre.	Bannya kempes.
I've lost my car keys.	Kunci mobilnya hilang.

BICYCLE / SEPEDA

Where can I hire a bicycle?	Saya bisa menyewa sepeda di mana?
Where can I find secondhand bikes for sale?	Sepeda bekas dijual di mana?
I've got a flat tyre.	Bannya pecah.
How much is it ...?	Berapa ongkosnya ...?
per hour	sejam
until (3 o'clock)	sampai (jam tiga)
the day	sehari

bike	sepeda
brakes	rem
to cycle	bersepeda
gears	gigi (also means 'teeth')
handlebars	gagang sepeda
helmet	helm
inner tube	ban dalam
lights	lampu
lock	kunci
pump	pompa
puncture	kebocoran/pecah
saddle	sadel
wheel	roda

LOCAL TRANSPORT — KENDARAAN LOKAL

There's a great variety of local transport in Indonesia. There's the becak, a bicycle-rickshaw found in many towns and cities across the nation. Increasingly, they're being banned from the central areas of major cities. There are none in Bali.

TRAVELLING SALESMEN

Whether on local transport or an inter-city bus, you'll soon realise that this is the domain of the country's many travelling salespeople and entertainers. Many buses stop frequently in villages to pick up more passengers, but will also pick up **penjual**, 'sellers', who roam the isles laden with their wares.

Some **penjual** simply call out what they have for sale. Others have a more elborate routine – they go down the aisle, dropping whatever they're selling into the lap of each passenger while extolling the benefits of their product and its price. It may be **permen jahe**, 'ginger sweets', **jamu**, 'herbal medicine', or even **kamus**, 'dictionaries'. So don't be surprised if a packet of **permen kopi**, 'coffee sweets' falls onto your lap. If you don't want to buy what's on offer, the **penjual** will be back to retrieve it; if you do, hand over the money instead.

Pemain musik, 'musicians', and **anak jalan**, 'street kids', make a living in the bigger cities by jumping onto buses, playing some tunes, then collecting money from passengers. Often the whole performance takes place while a bus is waiting at an intersection – the musician plays a few bars, waves a cup around for a collection then disappears in a cloud of pollution. Some musicians play their own compositions, complete with politically charged lyrics. Others play top-40 tunes, really badly.

The bajaj, a three-wheeler powered by a noisy two-stroke engine, is only found in Jakarta. In quieter towns, you may find andong and dokar – horse or pony carts with two (**dokar**) or four (**andong**) wheels.

With becak, bajaj and horse-carts, a price should be set before travel. Local transport will stop on request. If your fare hasn't been collected, give it to the driver.

Wait!	Tunggu!
I want to get off!	Kiri (depan)!; Stop!
Careful!	Hati-hati!
Danger!	Berbahaya!
Stop!	Stop!/Kiri!

AKOMODASI
ACCOMMODATION

Accommodation choices in Indonesia run the full gamut, from no-frills rumah penginapan, 'inns', to 5-star hotels.

The most traditional and commonly found type of accommodation is the losmen, 'inn' or 'guesthouse'. These are typically small and simple places, some with rooms with a kamar mandi, 'bathroom', some with AC, 'air-conditioning', some offering sarapan, 'breakfast' – no two are the same. Losmen are often family run, making them more homely places which are good for practising Indonesian. (See also Camping on page 151.)

FINDING ACCOMMODATION — MENCARI AKOMODASI

I'm looking for a ... — Saya mencari ...
- camping ground — tempat kemah
- guesthouse — losmen
- (upmarket) hotel — hotel (berbintang)

Where's a ... hotel? — Hotel yang ... di mana?
- cheap — termurah
- clean — bersih
- good — baik
- nearby — dekat

I've already found a hotel. — Saya sudah dapat hotel.
Please take me to the ... hotel. — Tolong antar saya ke hotel ...
What's the address? — Alamatnya bagaimana?
Could you write down the address, please? — Tolong tulis alamatnya?

The hotel is near the ... — Hotelnya dekat ...
- alley — gang
- beach — pantai
- shop — toko
- street — jalan
- town square — alun-alun

BOOKING AHEAD — PEMESANAN KAMAR

Can I book a room? — Boleh pesan kamar?
For (three) nights. — Selama (tiga) malam.

How much for ...? — Berapa harga ...?
- one night — satu malam
- a week — satu minggu
- two people — untuk dua orang

I'll/We'll be arriving ... — Saya/Kami tiba ...
- on the (3rd) — pada tanggal (tiga)
- later tonight — nanti malam

My name's ... — Nama saya ...

GOING POTTY!!

Although western-style toilets are becoming more common in hotels, squat toilets are still the norm. Toilet paper is rarely supplied, the left hand and water being the cleaning technique. There's often a bin supplied for paper and other waste, as flushing them often results in toilet blockage.

Where's the toilet? — Kamar kecil di mana?
I need to go! — Saya harus buang air!

toilet — kamar kecil; W C (pronounced *way say*)

CHECKING IN — MENDAFTARKAN DIRI

When finding a room, be sure to see it before deciding whether to take it. If you plan to stay a long time, you may be able to arrange a diskon, 'discount'.

I'd like a room for ...	Saya cari satu kamar untuk ... orang.
one person	satu
two people	dua
I'd like to share a dorm.	Saya cari satu kamar bersama orang lain.
I'd like a room with a ...	Saya cari satu kamar dengan ...
bathroom	kamar mandi
fan	kipas angin
shower	air dus
TV	TV
window	jendela
I'm going to stay for (one) ...	Saya menginap selama (satu) ...
day	hari
week	minggu
Is there a room available?	Ada kamar yang kosong?
Can I see the room?	Boleh saya melihat kamarnya?
I'm not sure how long I'm staying.	Saya belum tahu berapa lama saya menginap di sini.
I don't like this room.	Saya tidak suka kamar ini.
Do you have a better room?	Ada kamar yang lebih baik?
Do you have a room with ...?	Ada kamar dengan ...?
two beds	dua tempat tidur
a double bed	tempat tidur besar

Where's the bathroom?	Kamar mandi di mana?
Is there hot water all day?	Apakah air panas ada sepanjang hari?
Is breakfast included?	Apakah termasuk makan pagi?
This room's fine.	Kamar ini cocok.

THEY MAY SAY ...

Sudah penuh.	Sorry, we're full.
Berapa lama?	For how long?
Berapa malam/orang.	How many nights/people?
Termasuk teh/kopi.	It includes tea/coffee.
Bayar dulu.	Please pay now.
Bayar nanti.	Pay later.

Paying / Pembayaran

How much does it cost per day?	Berapa harganya sehari?
What's the daily rate?	Berapa harganya hariannya?
Does the price include breakfast/tax?	Apa harga termasuk sarapan/pajak?
Do you allow chidren?	Boleh saya bawa anak?
Is there extra cost for children?	Ada biaya tambahan untuk anak?
Can I pay by ...?	Bisa bayar dengan ...?
credit card	kartu kredit
travellers cheque	cek turis
Is there a discount for ...?	Ada diskon untuk ...?
children	anak
students	mahasiswa

REQUESTS & COMPLAINTS / PERMINTAHAN & KELUHAN

Do you have a safe where I can leave my valuables?	Ada tempat simpan barang berharga?
Could I have a receipt for them?	Minta kwitansi.
Where can I wash my clothes?	Di mana saya bisa mencuci pakaian?
Do you have a laundry service?	Ada servis cuci pakaian?
When will they be ready?	Kapan bisa diambil?
Can I use the telephone?	Boleh pakai telpon?
There are mosquitoes.	Ada nyamuk.
Do you have (a) ...?	Ada ...?
insect repellant	obat nyamuk
mosquito net	kelambu

KEEP IT CLEAN

Almost all Indonesian houses and many hotels don't have a western-style shower or bath. Instead, the kamar mandi, 'bathroom' (kamar meaning 'room' and mandi, 'bathe' or 'wash') includes a large trough-like vessel called a bak, used as an over-sized washbasin.

Don't ever get into the bak as if it were a bath, no matter how inviting it looks. Also, don't contaminate the water in the bak with sabun, 'soap'. There should be a gayung, 'pail' on hand with which you scoop water from the bak to throw over youself.

In remoter areas and in many villages, the kamar mandi is a section of the river. Privacy can never be assured and skilful sarong adjustments are the way to keep covered. Your technique will be scrutinised by an army of curious children.

This ... isn't clean.	... ini tidak bersih.
I need a(nother) ...	Saya perlu ... (lagi).
blanket	selimut
pillow	bantal
pillowcase	sarung bantal
sheet	seperai
Please change it/them.	Tolong ganti ini.
Please clean my room.	Tolong bersihkan kamar saya.
Excuse me, I've got a problem.	Ma'af, ada masalah.
The (window) is broken.	(Jendela)nya rusak.
I can't open/close the ...	Saya tidak bisa buka/tutup ...
door	pintunya
window	jendelanya
I can't lock the door.	Saya tidak bisa kunci pintunya.
I've locked myself out.	Kunci saya tertinggal di kamar.
Can you get it fixed?	Bisa diperbaiki?
The room is too ...	Kamarnya terlalu ...
cold	dingin
dark	gelap
hot	terlalu panas
noisy	ribut
smelly	berbau

THEY MAY SAY ...

Tidak apa-apa.	No worries.
Tidak usah.	No need.
Jangan repot.	Don't trouble yourself.
Jangan khawatir.	Don't worry.
Tidak ada masalah.	It's no problem.
Biar saja.	Let it be.

CHECKING OUT / MENINGGALKAN HOTEL

I'm leaving today.	Saya berangkat hari ini.
Please prepare my/our bill.	Tolong siapkan rekening saya/kami.
There's a mistake in the bill.	Rekeningnya salah.
Please call me a taxi.	Tolong panggilkan taksi.
Can I leave my things here until ...?	Bisa titip barang-barang saya sampai nanti ...?
this afternoon	siang
this evening	sore
tonight	malam

candle	lilin
chair	kursi
door	pintu
electricity	listrik
key	kunci
lamp	lampu
lock	kunci
mattress	kasur
mosquito coil	obat nyamuk
quiet	sepi
roof	atap
soap	sabun
toilet paper	kertas kloset
towel	handuk
to wake	bangun
wardrobe	lemari
... water	air ...
drinking	minum
hot	panas

LONGER STAYS — MENGINAP YANG LAMA

An alternative to hotels, if you plan to stay for at least a month, is to book a room in a kost. These are Indonesia's answer to share houses, and can be found near unversities and colleges.

A kost is a great place to meet locals. Rules and regulations sometimes apply, such as jam malam, 'curfew', and many are segregated into kost pria, 'men's accommodation' and kost wanita 'women's accommodation'.

GOOD SERVICE

We feel at home here.	Kami betah di sini.
It's comfortable here.	Nyaman di sini.
Thanks for your help.	Terima kasih atas bantuannya.

Is there a room available?	Ada kamar kosong?
I'm looking for a room near the beach/city-centre.	Saya cari kamar dekat pantai/pusat kota.
I want to rent a room/house for (three) months.	Saya mau menyewa kamar/ rumah selama (tiga) bulan.
I'm going to live here for a year.	Saya berencana tinggal di sini selama satu tahun.
How much per month?	Seminggu berapa ongkosnya?
to rent	menyewa

DI KOTA AROUND TOWN

LOOKING FOR ... MENCARI ...

How far's the ...?	Berapa jauh ...?
I'm going to the ...	Saya pergi ke ...
I'm looking for a/the ...	Saya mencari ...
bank	bank
barber	tukang cukur
consulate	konsulat
crossroad	perempatan
embassy	kedutaan besar
hairdresser	potong rambut; salon
hospital	rumah sakit
hotel	hotel/losmen
market	pasar
money changer	tempat penukaran uang
police station	kantor polisi
post office	kantor pos
public telephone	telepon umum; kios telpon; wartel
public toilet	WC umum
restaurant	rumah makan
school	sekolah
temple	candi/pura
town square	alun-alun; lapangan
village	desa/kampung
zoo	kebun binatang

What time does it open/close?	Jam berapa buka/tutup?
Is it still open?	Masih buka?

SIGNS

BUKA	OPEN
DILARANG ...	NO ...
MASUK	ENTRY
MEROKOK	SMOKING
DINGIN	COLD
DORONG	PUSH
KELUAR	EXIT
MASUK	ENTRANCE
PANAS	HOT
PRIA	MEN
TARIK	PULL
TUTUP	CLOSED
WANITA	WOMEN
WC	TOILETS

AT THE BANK — DI BANK

All tourist areas and large towns have money changers as well as banks. Tempat penukaran uang, 'money changers', can be more convenient, and usually have longer opening hours, but exchange rates and additional fees can vary dramatically.

Changing money in a bank can be a lengthy process, involving visits to a multitude of tellers. Anjungan Tunai Mandiri, 'Automatic Teller Machines' (ATMs), that recognise overseas cards have become commonplace in most cities.

The Indonesian currency is the rupiah (Rp) – 2000 rupiahs is written as Rp2000.

Can I exchange money here?	Bisa tukar uang?
Can I use my credit card to withdraw money?	Bisa dapat uang dengan kartu kredit?
Please write it down.	Tolong tuliskan.
Can I have smaller notes?	Minta uang kecil?
The ATM swallowed my card.	Kartu saya ditelan oleh ATMnya.

I want to change ...	Saya mau menukar ...
Australian dollars	dolar Australia
cash	uang kontan; duit
Pounds Stirling	Pounds Stirling
travellers cheques	cek turis
US dollars	dolar Amerika

THE LONG & THE SHORT

If you can't find a word in the dictionary, there's a good chance the word is a **singkatan**, 'abbreviation'. Indonesian is riddled with acronyms and word blends, and what's more, new ones are being created everyday.

ABG	**Anak Baru Gede** teenager (lit: child just-got big)
angkot	**angkutan kota** city transport
balita	**bawah lima tahun** a child under the age of five (lit: under five years)
deplu	**Departemen Luar Negri** Department of Foreign Affairs
monas	**Monumen Nasional** the National Monument (in Jakarta)
Puskesmas	**Pusat Kesehatan Masyarakat** local government health clinic
rubrik	**rumah fabrik** home-based factory or business (lit: house factory)
warteg	**warung Tegal** stall selling food from Tegal (lit: stall Tegal)
wartel	**warung telpon** telephone office

STREETLIFE

Exploring the streets of an Indonesian town can be both enthralling and exhausting. The traffic – both on and off the road – and the heat can all take their toll.

Then there's the attention you attract just by being there. The best way of saying no to someone persistently offering you services or products is to say: Terima kasih, 'Thanks but no thanks'.

Come here!	Ayo sini!
Go away!	Pergi!
I don't have any money.	Tidak ada uang.

alley	gang
beggar	pengemis; orang jalanan
footpath	pinggir jalan
hawker	penjual
thief	copet/maling
street	jalan
street kid	anak jalanan
street stall (food)	warung
traffic lights	lampu merah; lampu lalu-lintas

Where can I cash a travellers cheque?	Di mana saya bisa menguangkan cek turis?
What's the exchange rate?	Berapa kursnya?
Has any money arrived for me?	Ada kiriman uang untuk saya?
Can I transfer money here from my bank?	Bisakah mentransfer uang dari bank saya ke sini?
How long will it take?	Berapa lama prosesnya?
Do I have to pay commission?	Ada komisi?

bank clerk	pegawai bank
bank draft	surat wesel
branch	cabang
cash	uang kontan; duit
cashiers window	loket
cheque	cek
coins	uang logam; perak
commission	komisi
credit card	kartu kredit
endorsement	pengesahan
ID card	KTP (Kartu Tanda Penduduk)
letter of credit	surat kredit; LC
money	uang
note (bill)	uang kertas
signature	tanda tangan
teller	kasir

KNOW YOUR BIGWIGS

Remember to address officials as Pak, 'Sir', or Ibu, 'Ma'am'. In descending order of importance, official titles are:

head of a ...

province	Gubenur
regency	Bupati
district	Camat
village	Kepala desa/kampung

AT THE POST OFFICE — DI KANTOR POS

Kantor Pos, 'post offices', can be found in all towns. Larger post offices offer a variety of services including email and banking. The postal service is reliable yet slow. Poste restante is available, but be sure to check under both your first and last names. Postal services are also available from many tourist offices and **wartel/ warpostel**, 'telephone/postal offices'.

IN THE NEIGHBOURHOOD

At the front of a neighbourhood or village you may see an arch with the word **Dirgahayu RI** painted across it. This translates as 'Long Live the Republic of Indonesia', and the arch is built to celebrate Independence Day (see page 183).

Also in most neighbourhoods you'll find a small shelter with a large wooden bell hanging from the rafter. This is a **pos kamling** – short for **pos keamanan lingkungan**, 'neighbourhood safety post' – and is used as an emergency contact point. It also doubles as a place to meet and hang out.

I want to buy ...	**Saya mau membeli ...**
envelopes	**amplop**
postcards	**kartu pos**
stamps	**perangko**
I want to send a(n) ...	**Saya mau mengirim ...**
aerogram	**aerogram**
letter	**surat**
parcel	**paket**
telegram	**kawat/telegram**

Please send it (by) ... mail.	Tolong kirim dengan ...
air	pos udara.
express (domestic)	kilat (dalam negeri)
express (overseas)	ekspres (luar negeri)
registered	pos tercatat
surface	pos biasa

How much does it cost to send this to ...?	Berapa ongkos mengirim ini ke ...?
How much is an airmail letter to (the US)?	Berapa kalau kirim surat dengan pos udara ke (Amerika)?
Please send this parcel to (England) by surface mail.	Tolong kirimkan paket ini ke (Inggris) dengan pos biasa.
Please weigh this letter.	Tolong timbang surat ini.
Please stamp this letter immediately.	Tolong stempel surat ini.

glue	lem
mailbox	kotak pos
pen	pena
postage	perangko
postcode	kode pos
receiver (of a letter)	penerima
sender (of a letter)	pengirim
string	tali

PEACE CALL

Muslim Indonesians will often answer a call with the greeting **assalamualaikum** (lit: peace be on you).

TELECOMMUNICATIONS TELEKOMUNIKASI

As well as the larger telephone offices, **kantor telpon**, you can make calls from the smaller **wartel** and **kios telpon**.

Calls are charged by time, and prices vary depending on the time of day you call. Calling from a hotel can be exorbitantly expensive.

Could I please use the telephone?	**Boleh pakai telpon?**
What's the area code for ...?	**Nomor ... berapa?**
I want to call ...	**Saya mau menelpon ...**
The number is ...	**Nomornya ...**
I want to speak for (three) minutes.	**Saya mau bicara selama (tiga) menit.**
How much is a (three)-minute call to ..?	**Berapa rupiah (tiga) menit bicara ke ...?**
I want to make a reverse-charges phone call.	**Saya mau menelpon kolek.**
When's a cheap time to call?	**Jam berapa lebih murah untuk menelpon?**

Operator, I've been cut off.	Operator, sambungannya terputus.
The line is busy.	Telponnya sedang dipakai.
Sorry, you've got the wrong number.	Ma'af, nomornya salah.
Hello, do you speak English?	Halo, apakah Anda bisa bahasa Inggris?

PANCASILA

In government buildings, above cash registers in shops, on highway markers, at the end of television broadcasts, in the middle of television broadcasts and on school uniforms, you'll see the mythical form of the Garuda, the national symbol of Indonesia. On its breast are the five symbols of the Panca Sila, the 'five principles', which encompass the philosophical doctrine of Indonesia.

bintang
: a star representing faith in God, whether of Islamic, Christian, Buddhist, Hindu or of any other faith

rantai
: a chain representing humanity within Indonesian and its links to humankind as a whole

pohon beringin
: a banyan tree representing nationalism and promoting unity between Indonesia's many ethnic groups

kerbau
: a buffalo representing representative government

padi
: rice representing social justice

Making a Call — Menelepon

Hello.	Halo.
May I speak to ...?	Minta bicara dengan ...?
Who's calling?	Siapa ini?
This is ... speaking.	Ini ...
Yes, s/he's here.	Ya, dia ada.
One moment, please.	Tunggu sebentar.
I'm sorry, they're not here.	Ma'af, tidak ada.
What time will s/he be back?	Jam berapa dia pulang?
Can I leave a message?	Boleh titip pesan?
Please tell him/her I called.	Tolong beritahu dia saya telpon.
I'll call back later.	Nanti saya telpon lagi.

operator	Penghubung/Operator
phone book	buku telpon
phone box	boks telpon
phone call	panggilan telpon
phonecard	kartu telpon
reverse charges (collect)	kolek
telephone	telpon
to telephone	telpon
urgent call	telpon penting

THEY MAY SAY ...

Eren!	Cool!/Groovy!
Ngapain?	What's happening? (greeting)
Yuk!	Come on!; Follow me!
bule	westerner

Internet — Internet

Internet cafes have sprung up all over Indonesia in the past few years, offering cheap – yet sometimes slow – email access.

Is there a local Internet cafe?	Ada tempat email dekat di sini?
Where can I get access to the Internet?	Di mana saya bisa pakai internet?
What's the rate per hour?	Tarifnya sejam berapa?

BAD HAIR DAY

I'd like my hair cut.	Saya mau potong rambut.
Don't cut it too short.	Tolong jangan terlalu pendek.
I'd like my hair in the style of (Ricky Martin).	Saya mau gaya rambut (Ricky Martin).
Shave it all off!	Cukur sampai gundul!
I'd like my hair dyed ... (see page 125 for colours)	Saya mau rambut saya dicat ...
haircut	potong rambut
hairdressing salon	potong rambut; salon

SIGHTSEEING — TAMASYA

Where's the tourist office?	Kantor parawisata di mana?
What's that building?	Gedung itu gedung apa?
What's this monument?	Monumen ini monumen apa?
Who lived there?	Siapa dulu tinggal di sana?
Do you have a local map?	Apakah Anda punya peta setempat daerah ini?
Can I take (your) photo(s)?	Boleh ambil foto (Anda)?

I'll send you the photograph.	Nanti saya kirim foto kepada Anda.
Could you take a photo of me?	Tolong ambil foto saya.

TEMPLE TALK

kala	demonic face often seen over temple gateways
meru	shrines found in Balinese temples
pura dalem	Balinese temple of the dead
pura puseh	Balinese temple of origin
tau tau	life-sized carved wooden effigies of the dead placed outside cave graves in Sulawesi
temadu	carved ancestor totems
ura	Balinese temple or shrine

I want to see a/the ...	Saya mau lihat ...
I'd like to go to a/the ...	Saya mau ke ...
church	gereja
garden (botanical)	kebun (raya)
mosque	mesjid
museum	musium
nightclub	kelab malam
palace	istana
park	taman
performance	pertunjukan
public square	alun-alun; lapangan
royal palace	kraton
statue	patung
university	universitas

PAPERWORK — MENGISI FORMULIR

Most hotels will require you to fill in a guest form. If you need to have dealings with the Indonesian bureaucracy for any reason, you'll get further if you dress on the conservative side.

Forms — Formulir

name	nama
address	alamat
date/place of birth	tanggal/tempat lahir
age	umur
sex	jenis kelamin
nationality	kebangsaan
religion	agama
profession	pekerjaan

WHO'S YOUR GOD

Most official forms will ask your religion. Claiming to have no religion can create more attention than it's worth. So if you don't have one, take your pick:

Buddhist	Buda
Catholic	Katolik
Christian	Kristen
Hindu	Hindu
Jewish	Yahudi
Muslim	Muslim
Protestant	Protestan

marital status	status perkawinan
single	belum kawin
married	kawin
divorced	cerai
widow	janda
widower	duda
identification	surat keterangan
passport number	nomor paspor
visa	visa
birth certificate	surat keterangan lahir
drivers licence	SIM (Surat Izin Mengemudi)
reason for travel	maksud kunjungan
purpose of visit	maksud kunjungan
business	pekerjaan/bisnis
holiday	liburan
visiting relatives	kunjungan keluarga

HIBURAN DI LUAR RUMAH

GOING OUT

GOING OUT — HUBURAN DI LUAR RUMAH

Where to Go — Ke Mana

Once the sun sets over Indonesia, the most active places are night markets. There are bars and clubs in the main cities but, as in most countries, it takes persistence and luck to find the better ones.

DANGDUT

Western-style clubs keep popping up all over Indonesia, and although they can be fun, you could be just about anywhere. For an authentic night out, hunt down a **dangdut** bar.

Dangdut is a melange of traditional and modern music that originated in Indonesia but features instruments such as Indian tablas and flute. The result is sexy, love-drunk songs sung by heart-broken women or cheesy men, accompanied by straight-faced musos in matching suits. There's no denying that **dangdut** bars are sleazy – they're the domain of shady men and prostitutes. Saying that you're going to a **dangdut** bar may well destroy your reputation.

But the fact is, **dangdut** music is like no other. The beats are gutsy, the singing evocative and the emotions high. Going with a group of friends to a dangdut bar can be great night out, but leave your cool disposition at the door.

Asik!	Fantastic!
bergoyang	to writhe – what singers do on stage
kupu-kupu malam	prostitute (lit: night butterfly)

Most towns have a cinema. Just keep an eye out for Bombay-style, muscle-centric painted film posters.

Where's a …?	… di mana?
I'd like to go to a …	Saya mau ke …
bar	bar
nightclub	klub malam/disko
night market	pasar malam
I feel like …	Saya mau …
eating	makan
dancing	dansa
watching a film	menonton filem
I feel like going to a/the ...	Saya mau lihat ...
cinema	bioskop
concert	konser
puppet show	pertunjukan wayang kulit
theatre	sandiwara/teater

SHADOW PUPPETS

cempala	wooden mallet used in performance
dalang	puppeteer
gamelan	orchestra which accompanies a wayang kulit show
kayon	leaf-shaped device used to end scenes or to symbolise wind, mountains, obstacles, clouds or the sea
kendang	drum
lakon	drama taken from a legend performed in a wayang kulit performance
wayang kulit	shadow puppets

Invites / Undangan

Would you like to go to a cinema with me?	Apakah Anda mau ke bioskop dengan saya?
Do you know a good club?	Apakah Anda tahu di mana ada klub yang baik?
I'll pay.	Saya bayar.
Come along.	Ikut.
The night's young!	Masih sore!

Responding to Invites / Membalas Undangan

I'd like to.	Ya/Boleh.
I can't.	Tidak bisa.

THEY MAY SAY ...

Begitu!	It's like that!
Benar!	True!
Betul!	That's right!
Bukan main!	No joke!
Masak!	Really!
Wah!	Wow!
Ya Allah!	Oh my God!
Ya ampun!	No way!

Nightclubs & Bars / Klub Malam & Bar

How should we get there?	Naik apa ke sana?
Are these clothes OK?	Pakaian ini cocok?
Is there an admission charge?	Ada harga masuk?
What sort of music do you like?	Anda suka musik apa?
Do you like this music?	Apakah Anda suka musik ini?
I like techno.	Saya suka tekno.
Let's dance.	Ayo dansa.

This place is ...	Tempat ini ...
That person's ...	Dia ...
cool	keren
sleazy	genit
strange	aneh

Let's go somewhere else.	Ayo ke tempat lain.

INDONESIAN RHYTHMS

In addition to all the western hits, you'll find a huge range of traditional and modern local music in Indonesia.

alternatif
alternative, complete with grunt and distortion

dangdut
passionate and sexy sounds (see page 99)

gamelan
an orchestra consisting mainly of percussion instruments (gongs, drums, xylophones) but can also include vocals and flute. The set-up and tempo varies from region to region.

jaipongan
a blend of traditional instruments and modern rhythm incorporating strong and complex rhythm on the **kendang**, 'drum'. **Jaipongan** is considered rather risque.

kacapi suling
serene music featuring **kacapi**, a harp-like instrument, **suling**, 'flute', and singing

popular
popular music, complete with hype, shlock and over-production

DATING & ROMANCE — BERPACARAN

Looking for a Date? — Cari Pacar?

Would you like to get together ...?	Apakah Anda mau bersama saya ...?
again	lagi
later tonight	nanti malam
tomorrow	besok

I'd like to.	Ya./Boleh.
No thanks.	Terima kasih (pol); Tidak(inf)
Go away.	Pergi.
Don't hassle me.	Jangan ganggu.

I have a ...	Saya punya ...
boyfriend/girlfriend	pacar
husband	suami
wife	isteri

NARKOTICA

Narcotics are illegal in Indonesia and penalties can be severe, even for possession.

cocaine	kokain
ecstasy	ekstasi
heroin	heroin
marijuana	ganja
speed	sabu-sabu

BALINESE DANCE

Baris
: energetic warrior dance in which a solo dancer interprets the thoughts and emotions of a warrior as he prepares for battle and meets the enemy

Barong & Rangda
: depicts two characters personifying good and evil. The Barong Keket, a half dog, half lion character played by two men, protects the local village from rangda, a witch, in a battle in which good eventually triumphs over evil.

Janger
: a chorus of women sway and chant while men perform a dance involving shouting and violent movement

Kebyar
: male solo dance

Kecak
: accompanied by a chanting choir, the kecak tells the tale of the Ramayana, the quest of a prince to rescue his wife from a kidnapping king

Legong
: the Legong has various forms, of which Legong Kraton, 'Legong of the palace', is the most popular. Three dancers relate the story of a king who takes a woman captive, only to be killed in battle by her brother.

Pendet
: dance performed before making temple offerings

Ramayana
: similar to the Kecak, but embellished with improvisation and comedy

Sanghyang
: two women dancing a dream-like version of the Legong, performed with eyes shut and background choir chanting

Topeng
: masked dance where dancers imitate the characters portrayed by their masks

Love / Cinta

You're beautiful (m/f). — Kamu ganteng/cantik.
You're sexy. — Kamu seksi.
I'm feeling sexy. — Saya terangsang.
Let's kiss. — Mari ciuman.
Let's make love. — Mari kita main cinta.
Do you have a condom? — Ada kondom?

No condom, no sex. — Tidak boleh tanpa kondom.
(Don't) stop! — (Jangan) berhenti!
Delicious! — Enak!
Out of this world! — Luar biasa!
Do you want to smoke? — Anda mau rokok?
Can I stay? — Boleh saya menginap?
Can I see you again? — Apakah kita bisa bertemu lagi?
I'll call you. — Nanti saya telpon.
Do you want to be my girlfriend/boyfriend? — Apakah Anda mau jadi pacar saya?

KEEPING COOL

Let it be. — Biar saja.
Don't worry. — Jangan kawatir.
Don't trouble yourself. — Jangan repot.
No worries. — Tidak apa apa.
It's no problem. — Tidak ada masalah.
No need. — Tidak usah.

STUBBED YOUR TOE?

All these words can be used to mean 'Dammit!'.

Anjing!	(lit: dog!)
Celaka!	(lit: misfortune!)
Sebel!	(lit: resent!)
Setan!	(lit: satan!)

Leaving & Breaking Up — Memutuskan Pacar

I leave tomorrow. — Besok saya berangkat.
I'll miss you. — Saya akan rindu Anda.
Let's keep in touch. — Harap kita tetap berkomunikasi.

This relationship isn't appropriate. — Hubungan ini tidak cocok.

QUESTIONS PERTANYAAAN

Whether in a bemo 'minibus' or someone's home, you'll almost certainly be asked questions about yourself and the members of your family, in particular:

Sudah kawin?	Are you married?

Unless you're indeed married, the appropriate answer is:

Belum.	Not yet.

WHO'S YER FATHER?

As well as meaning 'father', the word **bapak** can be used when addressing any older male (see Forms of Address, page 43). When referring to your biological father, you can use the term **ayah**.

Although tidak, 'no', would be grammatically fine to use, many Indonesians wouldn't understand why you're not already married, or at least thinking about it. You'll avoid unwarranted concern, especially if you're a woman, if you answer sudah, 'already' or belum, 'not yet'.

As it isn't generally considered normal for unmarried couples in Indonesia to be travelling and/or living together, you'll attract less attention if you say you're married.

Do you have a boyfriend/girlfriend?	Sudah punya pacar?
Is your husband/wife here?	Suami/Isteri Anda di sini?
Do you have any brothers and sisters?	Punya kakak atau adik?

How many brothers and sisters do you have?	Berapa saudara Anda?
Do you have any children?	Sudah punya anak?
How many children do you have?	Berapa anak?

MAKING A NAME

You can create a noun from many root words by adding the suffix -an to the root.

Root Word		Noun	
bite	gigit	a bite	gigitan
swing	buai	hammock	buaian

REPLIES — BALASAN

I'm not married yet.	Saya belum nikah/kawin.
I'm single.	Saya belum kawin.
I'm married.	Saya sudah nikah/kawin.
I don't have any children.	Saya tidak punya anak.
I don't have any children yet.	Saya belum punya anak.
This is my ...	Ini ... saya.
I have ...	Saya punya ...
one son	satu anak laki-laki
three sons	tiga anak laki-laki
one daughter	satu anak perempuan
three daughters	tiga anak perempuan
I have two younger brothers.	Saya punya dua adik laki-laki.

NYA NYA NYA

The suffix -nya (lit: of-him/her) is affixed to a noun to indicate that something is 'his' or 'hers'.

his jacket	jaket-nya (lit: jacket-of-him)
her money	uang-nya (lit: money-of-her)

It can also be used in place of the plural possessive mereka, 'their'.

their house	rumah-nya (lit: house-of-them)

Another use of -nya is in the same way that English speakers use the definite article 'the'.

I'm going to the office	Saya ke kantornya.

In other words, depending on context, -nya can mean 'the', 'of-him/her', 'of-them'.

FAMILY MEMBERS — ANGGOTA KELUARGA

Brothers and sisters are always referred to as being either older or younger.

aunt	tante/bibi
boyfriend	pacar
child(ren)	anak(-anak)
cousin	sepupu
daughter	anak perempuan
family	keluarga
father	bapak/ayah
friend	teman
girlfriend	pacar

grandchild	cucu
grandfather	kakek
grandmother	nenek
husband	suami
mother	ibu
older/younger brother	kakak/adik laki-laki
older/younger sister	kakak/adik perempuan
partner	pasangan
son	anak laki-laki
uncle	paman/om
wife	isteri

COMMON INTERESTS — MINAT BERSAMA

What do you do in your spare time?	Anda suka main apa?
What hobby do you have?	Apa hobi Anda?
I (don't) like ...	Saya (tidak) suka ...
Do you like ...?	Apakah Anda suka ...?
art	seni
cooking	masak
dancing (traditional)	tari
dancing (contemporary)	dansa
discos	disko
film	filem
going out	berjalan-jalan
going shopping	berbelanja
music	musik
photography	fotografi
playing sport	berolahraga
reading books	membaca buku
the theatre	sandiwara/teater
travelling	bepergian
watching TV	menonton televisi
writing	menulis

KKN

KKN, which stands for Kolusi, Korupsi, Nepotisme, 'Collusion, Corruption, Nepotism' became one of the buzz words of the post-Soeharto reform era.

SPORT OLAHRAGA

Indonesians are big on sport, especially bulutangkis, 'badminton' and sepak bola, 'soccer'. Indonesian badminton players rank among the best in the world, and the national soccer league has a passionate following complete with pitch invasions and impromptu fireworks. When a gol, 'goal' is scored, it's appropriate to scream masuk, 'enter' or, as in all soccer-mad nations:

goooooooooooooaaaaaaal!

Early-morning exercise regimens are also common, and being woken by 50 old folk in matching tracksuits, moving in sync to a top-40 hit, isn't a rare occurrence.

PENCAK SILAK

Although lacking in the noteriety of kung fu, karate and taikwando, Indonesia has its own style of martial arts – pencak silat, 'the beauty of fighting'.

Originally from Sumatra, the popularity of pencak silat has spread across the archipelago, and individual regions have developed their own distinct styles. Competitions take place throughout Indonesia, and nowadays, even internationally. Although styles may differ, unifying rules and techniques make such competitions possible.

The study of pencak silat can be divided into three broad areas – olahraga, 'sport', kesenian, 'art' and tenaga dalam, 'inner power'. The 'inner power' facet involves mind control and strength. Pencak silat is a recognised part of national school curriculum, and also offered at many universities.

Pencak silat can also be performed to music, with routines encompassing key steps and transitions. Performances can incorporate weaponry or ornamental fans. In some regions, competitions and performances are carried out at weddings, harvest festivals and circumcision ceremonies.

Do you like sport?	Anda suka main olahraga?
I like playing sport.	Saya suka main olahraga.
I prefer to watch rather than play sport.	Saya lebih senang menonton daripada main olahraga.
Do you play ...?	Anda bisa main ...?
Would you like to play/go/do ...?	Apakah Anda mau main ...?
badminton	bulutangkis
baseball	baseball
basketball	bola basket
boxing	tinju
diving	selam
football (soccer)	sepak bola
gymnastics	senam
hockey	hoki
keeping fit	menjaga kesehatan
martial arts	bela diri
rugby	rugby
skiing	main ski
soccer	sepak bola
surfing	berselancar
swimming	berenang
table tennis	tenis meja
tennis	tenis

CAN'T MAKE UP YOUR MIND?

I don't know.	Saya tidak tahu.
I'm undecided.	Saya ragu-ragu.
I'm not sure.	Saya tidak yakin.
I've changed my mind.	Saya merubah rencana.
I was wrong.	Saya salah.

PLAYTIME

The word main (lit: play) is a word you'll hear in many situations.

Come visit my home at any time.	Kapan saja main di rumah saya.
We're just joking.	Kami main-main saja.
S/he's flirting. (lit: s/he playing eyes)	Dia main mata.
The show has started.	Pertunjukan sudah main.
Do you like to play sport?	Suka main olahraga?

WRITING LETTERS — MENULIS SURAT

Once you get back home, you may want to drop a line to people you met. Here are a few lines to help.

Dear ...,	Kepada ... yang baik,
I'm sorry it's taken me so long to write.	Mohon ma'af sudah lama saya tidak mengirim surat.
It was great to meet you.	Saya senang sekali kita dapat bertemu.
Thanks so much for your hospitality.	Terima kasih atas keramah-tamaan Anda.
I miss you (sg/pl).	Saya rindu Anda/kalian.
I had a fantastic time in ...	Pengalaman saya di ... luar biasa.
My favourite place was ...	... ialah tempat yang paling saya sukai.
I hope to visit ... again.	Semoga saya bisa mengunjungi ... lagi.
Say 'hi' to ... and ... for me.	Tolong sampaikan salam kepada ... dan ...
I'd love to see you again.	Saya ingin sekali bertemu dengan Anda lagi.
Write soon!	Tulislah!
With love/regards,	Dengan cinta/hormat,

SOCIAL ISSUES — ISU SOSIAL

Recent social and political upheaval in Indonesia has meant people are much more open about discussing politics and other social issues.

This freedom of expression has resulted in a wave of new words entering everyday Indonesian. Many words and concepts have been adapted from English, so with a keen eye and ear you'll be able to decipher slogans, banners and graffiti.

What do people/you think about ...?	Rakyatnya/Anda pikir apa tentang ...?
I (don't) agree.	Saya (tidak) setuju.
Do you like ...?	Apakah Anda suka ...?
I (don't) like ...	Saya (tidak) suka ...
Really?; Is that so?	Masak?
Really!	Betul!
I support the ... party.	Saya mendukung partai ...
In my country, we have a conservative/liberal government.	Pemerintah di negara saya konservatif/liberal.

PATRIOTISME

Indonesia Raya	Indonesia the Great (the national anthem)
Tanah Air	Land & Water (lit: native land)
Merah Putih	Red & White (refers to the Indonesian flag)
Merdeka!	Free/Independent! (a revolutionary cry)

COME TO THE PARTAI!

Indonesian elections have seen up to 48 parties vying for the top job. Some parties are denominational, some are left-wing, some aren't, but all have funky symbols.

Golkar (Golongan Karya)	Working Party
PAN (Partai Amanat Nasional)	National Mandate Party
PDI-P (Partai Demokratik Indonesia Perjuangan)	Indonesian Democratic Party of Struggle
PKB (Partai Kebangkitan Bangsa)	Rising National Party

POLITICS — POLITIK

cronyism	kronisme
demonstration/rally	demo
democracy	demokrasi
dual function (referring to the function of the military – defence *and* politics)	dwi fungsi
general election	pemilihan umum
government	pemerintah
Indonesian Armed Forces	ABRI (Angkatan Bersenjata Republik Indonesia)
Indonesian Army	TNI (Tentara Nasional Indonesia)
monetary crisis	krismon (krisis moniter)

Parliament — DPR (Dewan Perwakilan Rakyat)
(lit: council representing the people)

policy — kebijaksanaan
politician — politikus
President — Presiden

... reformation — reformasi ...
peaceful/total — damai/total

revolution — revolusi
socialism — sosialisme

IDIOMS

Ada gula ada semut.
(lit: where there's sugar there are ants)
Like bees to the honey pot.

Tiada gading yang tak retak.
(lit: there's no ivory that isn't cracked)
No one's perfect.

Nasi sudah menjadi bubur.
(lit: the rice has already become porridge)
You can't turn the clock back.

Tong kosong nyaring bunyinya.
(lit: an empty barrel resounds loudly)
Empty vessels make the most noise.

Karena nila setitik rusak susu sebelanga.
(lit: a drop of indigo ruins the pot of milk)
A bad apple spoils the barrel.

USEFUL WORDS

economy	ekonomi
exploitation	exploitasi
history	sejarah
justice	keadilan
the people	rakyat
poverty	kemiskinan
riot	kerusuhan
transmigration (migration within Indonesia)	transmigrasi
unemployment	pengangguran
welfare	kesejahteraan
worker	buruh

LOOKING FOR ... / MENCARI ...

Where's a/the ...?	... di mana?
bakery	Toko roti
barber	Tukang cukur rambut
bookshop	Toko buku
camera shop	Toko kamera
chemist	Apotik
clothing store	Toko pakaian
general store	Toko umum/swalayan
grocery	Toko makanan
kiosk	Kios (see box on page 129)
market	Pasar
music store	Toko musik
night market	Pasar malam
shopping centre	Pusat pertokoan
souvenir shop	Toko oleh-oleh
supermarket	Pasar swalayan
tailor	Penjahit

MAKING A PURCHASE / MEMBELI SESUATU

Where can I buy ...?	... dijual di mana?
Do you have any ...?	Ada ...?
I'm looking for (a) ...	Saya cari ...
I'm just looking.	Saya lihat-lihat saja.
How much is it?	Berapa harganya?
How much is this?	Berapa harga ini?
Can you write down the price?	Tolong tulis harganya.
Do you accept credit cards?	Bisa bayar dengan kartu kredit?

THEY MAY SAY ...

Bisa saya bantu?	Can I help you?
Cari apa?	What are you looking for?
Ada, sebentar.	We've got that, just a moment.
Warna apa?	What colour?
Apakah ini baik?	Is this what you're looking for?
Harganya dua puluh ribu rupiah.	The price is Rp20,000.
Tidak ada.	We don't have any

Can I try this on?	Boleh saya coba?
Do you have others?	Ada yang lain?
Where are these made?	Barang-barang ini dibuat di mana?
Can I see it?	Boleh saya lihat?
I don't like it.	Saya tidak suka ini.
It's beautiful!	Indah sekali!
I'll take it.	Saya beli ini.

BARGAINING — TAWAR-MENAWAR

Bargaining is an intrinsic part of life in Indonesia. Everybody does it, not just tourists. Although it can be tiresome, it's helpful to think of bargaining as the art of compromise, requiring patience and a little charm. Be sure you want the item before you start bargaining, and remember not to get worked up over a paltry sum.

You can bargain for most things in Indonesia. Consider it obligatory in markets, souvenir stalls, and for becaks and unmetered taxis.

It's too expensive.	Terlalu mahal.
Can you lower the price?	Boleh kurang?
I'll give you ...	Saya bayar ...
No more/less than ...	Tidak lebih/kurang dari ...
This is my final offer.	Ini tawaran terakhir saya.

cheap	murah
discount	korting/diskon
expensive	mahal

ALL WRAPPED UP

batik	patterned fabric dyed using wax
gringsing	Balinese double ikat woven cloth
ikat	material woven from tie-dyed thread
songket	silk cloth interwoven with silver or gold thread

DRIVING A HARD BARGAIN

Pembeli: ('Buyer') Excuse me (ma'am), how much is this?
Permisi (Ibu), berapa harganya?

Penjual: ('Seller') The price is Rp50,000.
Harganya lima puluh ribu rupiah.

Pb: Woah, that's expensive!
Wah, mahal!

Pj: I can lower the price.
Bisa kurang sedikit.

Pb: How about Rp25,000?
Bagaimana kalau dua puluh lima ribu rupiah?

Pj: Lordy! I'll be at a loss. It's good quality.
Aduh! Saya rugi. Kwalitasnya baik.

Pb: Yes, it's very beautiful, but the price is too high.
Ya indah sekali, tetapi harganya terlalu tinggi.

Pj: OK, how about just Rp40,000.
OK, empat puluh ribu rupiah saja.

Pb: I'll pay no more than Rp30,000.
Saya bayar tidak lebih dari tiga puluh ribu rupiah.

Pj: Wow, your Indonesian is great! Rp35,000?
Wah bahasa Indonesia Anda bagus! Tiga puluh lima ribu rupiah?

Pb: Alright.
Boleh.

ESSENTIAL ITEMS / BARANG YANG PERLU

I'm looking for (a) ...	Saya cari ...
batteries	baterai
bread (often sweet & spongy)	roti
butter	mentega
cheese	keju
chocolate	coklat
eggs	telur
flour	tepung
ham	daging babi
honey	madu
margarine	mentega
matches	korek api
milk	susu
toilet paper	kertas kloset; tisu
toothpaste	tapal gigi
torch (flashlight)	senter
towel	handuk
washing powder	pembersih/deterjen
yogurt	yogurt; susu masam kental

SOUVENIRS / OLEH-OLEH

basket	keranjang
... batik	batik ...
handmade/printed	tulis/cap
bracelet	gelang
cane ware	rotan
... carving	ukiran ...
stone/wood	batu/kayu
earrings	anting-anting
handcrafts	kerajinan tangan
jewellery	perhiasan
machete	mandau

carved masks	topeng
material (fabric)	kain
necklace	kalung
ornamental knives	kris
paintings	lukisan
pottery	keramik
... puppets	wayang ...
shadow/wooden	kulit/golek
ring	cincin
sarong	sarung
shell	kerang
statue	patung

CLOTHING — PAKAIAN

bra	beha
cardigan	mantel
dress	baju
gloves	sarung tangan
hat	topi
jacket	jaket
jeans	jean
jumper	kaos hangat
pants	celana panjang
raincoat	jas hujan
sandals	sandal
shirt	kemeja
shoelaces	tali sepatu
shoes	sepatu
shorts	celana pendek
skirt	rok
socks	kaos kaki
swimsuit	pakaian renang
tie	dasi
trousers	celana panjang
T-shirt	kaos
underwear	celana dalam

MATERIALS — BAHAN

bone	tulang
cotton	katun
gold	emas
jackfruit wood	buah nangka
leather	kulit
rattan	rotan
sandalwood	cendana
shell	kerang
silk	sutra
silver	perak
wood	kayu
wool	wol

LOST THE THREAD?

buttons	kancing
needle	jarum
scissors	gunting
thread	benang

COLOURS — WARNA

black	hitam
blue	biru
brown	coklat
dark ...	... tua
green	hijau
grey	abu-abu
light ...	... muda
multicoloured	berwarna-warna
orange	oranye/jingga
pink	merah muda
purple	ungu
red	merah
white	putih
yellow	kuning

TOILETRIES	PERLENGKAPAN MANDI
comb	sisir
condoms	kondom
contraceptive	kontrasepsi
deodorant	deodoran
laxative	obat cuci perut
moisturising cream	krim pelembab
mosquito repellent	obat nyamuk
razor	pisau cukur
razor blade	silet
sanitary napkins	duk/softex
shampoo	sampo; pencuci rambut
shaver	pisau cukur
shaving cream	krim cukur
soap	sabun
sunblock cream	krim penahan matahari
tampons	tampon
tissues	tisu
toothbrush	sikat gigi

FOR THE BABY	UNTUK BAYI
baby's bottle	botol bayi
baby food (tinned)	makanan bayi (kaleng)
baby powder	bedak bayi
bib	oto
disposable nappies (diapers)	popok
dummy (pacifier)	dot
nappy rash cream	krem ruam (untuk bayi)
powdered milk	susu bubuk
sling used for carrying a baby	selendang

STATIONERY & PUBLICATIONS — ALAT TULIS-MENULIS & PENERBITAN

Is there an English-language bookshop here?	Ada toko buku bahasa Inggris?
Is there an English-language section?	Ada bagian bahasa Inggris?
Do you sell ...?	Apakah ... dijual?
envelopes	amplop
magazines	majalah
(English-language) newspapers	koran (bahasa Inggris)
novels	novel/roman
pens	pena
postcards	kartu pos
stamps	perangko
writing paper	kertas tulis
... dictionaries	kamus ...
bilingual	dua bahasa
pocket	kecil
... maps	peta ...
city	kota
regional	daerah
road	jalan

PERMISI

Permisi is a useful word that can be used to attract service in a shop or to get someone's attention. It's also handy for trying to get through the crowd in a busy market, or when entering or leaving someone's room or home. It's a polite and effective way of being heard.

MUSIC — MUSIK

I'm looking for a ... CD.	Saya mencari CD ...
Do you have ...?	Ada ...?
What's the best dangdut recording?	Apa CD dangdut yang paling baik?
I heard a band/singer called ...	Saya mendengarkan band/ penyanyi bernama ...
Can I listen to this CD here?	Bisa mendengarkan CD di sini?
I want a blank tape.	Saya mau kaset kosong.

(See Going Out, page 102, for styles of music.)

THE LYING CAMERA

It's good to remember that a camera and printing costs are very expensive for many Indonesians. As a result, taking photos is often seen not as a way to catch a candid moment, but as a chance to document a special occasion.

This may explain why, when taking a photo of an Indonesian friend in their home, their warm smile may be replaced with the straight-faced stare of a mug shot. Shouting keju, 'cheese' won't help things. The exception to this is with young boys, many of whom enjoy striking some sort of kung-fu-cum-rock-star pose at the sight of a camera.

Can I take a photo (of you)?	Boleh saya potret?
Can I take a photo (of that)?	Boleh saya potret tu?
I'll send you a copy.	Saya mengirim potretnya.

PHOTOGRAPHY / FOTOGRAFI

I'd like a film for this camera.	Saya mau filem untuk kamera ini.
How much is it for processing and developing?	Berapa ongkosnya cuci cetak?
When will it be ready?	Siap jam berapa?
Do you repair cameras here?	Bisa memperbaiki kamera di sini?

battery	baterai
B&W (film)	(filem) hitam putih
camera	kamera
colour (film)	(filem) berwarna
to develop	cuci
film	filem
flash(bulb)	balon lampu
lens	lensa
light meter	meteran cahaya
photograph	foto
to print	cetak
slides	slide
videotape	video kaset

ONE STOP SHOPPING

On nearly every street corner you'll find a small stall, its windows crowded with botol, 'bottles', rokok, 'cigarettes', permen, 'sweets' and other products. This is a kios, 'kiosk', and although tiny, each kios has a phenomenal storage capacity, with many even stocking alcohol and pharmaceutical goods.

So, buy your beer, smokes and obat kepala sakit 'headache pills', here.

SMOKING — MEROKOK

This is a national pastime, although many women only smoke inside the home. The smell of a kretek, 'clove cigarette', is synonymous with Indonesia.

A packet of cigarettes, please.	Minta rokok satu bungkus.
Do you have a light?	Minta api.
Are these cigarettes strong or mild?	Apakah rokok ini keras atau ringan?
Do you mind if I smoke?	Boleh merokok di sini?
Please don't smoke.	Harap jangan merokok.
I'm trying to give up.	Saya sedang berhenti merokok.

cigarette papers	kertas rokok
cigarettes	rokok
clove cigarette	kretek
filter	filter
lighter	geretan/api
matches	korek api
menthol	mentol
pipe	pipa rokok
smoke	asap
to smoke	rokok
tobacco	tembakau

HEADDRESSING

The head covering you'll see worn by many Muslim women is called a jilbab.

SIZES & COMPARISONS — UKURAN & PERBANDINAGAN

a little bit	sedikit
many	banyak
too much/many	terlalu banyak
enough	cukup
big	besar
bigger	lebih besar
biggest	paling besar
very big	sangat besar
too big	terlalu besar
small	kecil
smaller	lebih kecil
smallest	paling kecil
less	kurang
more	lebih banyak
heavy	berat
light	ringan
long	panjang
short	pendek
tall	tinggi
wide	lebar
narrow	sempit

WEIGHTS & MEASURES — BERAT &UKURAN

millimetre	milimeter
centimetre	sentimeter
metre	meter
kilometre	kilometer
litre	liter
gram	gram
kilogram	kilogram

USEFUL WORDS	KATA YANG BERGUNA
to buy	membeli
cheap	murah
to export	mengekspor
to import	mengimpor
made in	dibuat di
old	tua/lama
to order	memesan
quality	kwalitas/mutu
quantity	jumlah
round (shape)	bulat
to sell	menjual
type (of product)	macam/jenis

MAKANAN FOOD

For many visitors to Indonesia, local food means nasi goreng and gado-gado, and understandably they soon long for variety.

The variety is there if you explore a little deeper, ask what things are, and eat where the locals eat – at street stalls, roving vendors, and night markets that spring up when the sun goes down.

breakfast	makan pagi; sarapan
lunch	makan siang
dinner	makan malam

DID YOU KNOW ...

Indonesians don't use chopsticks – many don't use cutlery at all. Instead they pakai tangan, 'use their right hand'.

VEGETARIAN & SPECIAL MEALS — MAKANAN NABATI & MAKANAN ISTIMEWA

If you're a vegetarian, you can specify tanpa daging, without meat, or sayur saja, vegetables only.

I'm a vegetarian.	Saya hanya makan sayuran.
I don't/can't eat ...	Saya tidak suka /tahan makan ...
chicken	ayam
eggs	telur
fish	ikan
ham	daging babi; ham
meat	daging
milk and cheese	susu dan keju
prawns	udang

I'm allergic to ...	Saya alergi kalau makan ...
dairy products	susu
peanuts	kacang
Do you have any vegetarian dishes?	Ada makanan nabati?
Does this dish have meat/chicken?	Apakah ada daging/ayam dalam masakan ini?
Can I get this without meat/chicken?	Bisa tanpa daging/ayam?
Does it contain eggs?	Apakah mengandung telur?

Kosher restaurants are unknown in Indonesia, but halal restaurants use no pork products.

Is there a halal restaurant here?	Ada rumah makan halal di sini?
Is this halal?	Apakah ini halal?

THEY MAY SAY ...

Makan apa?	What would you like to eat?
Minim apa?	What would you like to drink?

EATING OUT — MAKAN DI LUAR

Where's a ... ?	... di mana?
food stall	warung
night market	pasar malam
roving vendor	kaki lima
Where's a ... restaurant?	Rumah makan ... di mana?
cheap	murah
Padang (see box on page 136)	Padang

We'd like a table for (five), please.	Minta meja untuk (lima) orang.
I want to eat ...	Saya mau makan ...
What dish is that?	Itu masakan apa?
What's in that dish?	Masakan itu apa isinya?
Is it spicy?	Pedas?
How much does one portion cost?	Berapa harga satu porsi?
We're in a hurry. Please bring our food quickly.	Kami terburu-buru. Tolong bawa makanan secepat-cepatnya.
Do I get it myself or do they bring it to us?	Apakah ambil sendiri atau dilayani?

DID YOU KNOW ...

The city of Yogyakarta is also known as Kota Gudeg, in honour of the regional speciality, a jackfruit and coconut curry.

Please bring a/an/the ...	Minta ...
ashtray	asbak
bill	bon
cup	cangkir
fork	garpu
glass	gelas
glass of water (with/without ice)	segelas air putih (dengan/tanpa es)
knife	pisau
menu	daftar makanan
plate	piring
spoon	sendok
toothpick	tusuk gigi

PADANG FOOD

One of the most popular types of eateries is a rumah makan Padang, 'Padang restaurant', named after the Sumatran city.

Many visitors steer clear of Padang food as it's pre-cooked and displayed in a window. But with such a high turnover, the food remains fresh and the spices preserve the food well.

Just point to the dishes you want (three is usually enough) and they'll be served to you with rice. Some restaurants bring an assortment of dishes to the table and you pay for what you eat.

Choosing a meat dish will double the price. Portions are small but tasty, rice being the filler.

This isn't cooked properly.	**Ini masih mentah.**
Not too spicy please.	**Jangan terlalu pedas.**
No MSG please.	**Tolong jangan pakai vetsin.**
No ice, please.	**Tanpa es, terima kasih.**

This is (too) ...	**Makanan ini (terlalu) ...**
bitter	**pahit**
cold	**dingin**
delicious	**enak**
fresh	**segar**
hot	**panas**
salty	**asin**
sour	**asam**
spicy	**pedas**
spoiled	**busuk**
stale	**busuk**
sweet	**manis**
unripe	**mentah**
uncooked	**mentah**

TYPICAL DISHES — MAKANAN BIASA

Many eateries don't have menus – what's available is usually advertised on the wall, the stall tarpaulin or the side of the kaki-lima, 'footpath'.

The names of many dishes specify how they're prepared, such as ayam bakar, 'grilled chicken'. The general term sayur is often used to describe vegetable dishes such as kangkung.

MEALS ON LEGS

Delicious food is available from roving food vendors known as kaki lima (lit: five legs – two wheels, a stand plus the legs of the cook). Each kaki lima has a particular sound, depending on what's being sold. Listen for the cry of bakso!, or the wooden *tock* on the sate seller's bell.

Main Course — Makanan Utama

asinan	raw vegetables, salted
ayam	chicken (small by western standards, but big on taste – no hormones!)
ayam ...	... chicken
bakar	grilled
goreng	fried
babi	pig
bakmi/ba'mi	rice noodles
bakso/ba'so	meatball soup
bala bala	vegetable fritter
bebek	duck
bubur ayam	chicken porridge
bubur kacang hijau	mung bean porridge
cakar ayam	chicken claw (the tastiest part)
cumi-cumi	squid
cap cai	stirfried vegetables (Chinese dish)
daging sapi	beef
domba	lamb/mutton
gado-gado	cooked vegetables with peanut sauce
gudeg	chicken or egg cooked and served with jackfruit and coconut (Yogyakarta speciality)
hati	liver
ikan (tambak/laut)	(freshwater/saltwater) fish
jagung bakar	roasted corn
jantung	heart
kambing	goat
kangkung	water spinach
kari	curry
kelinci	rabbit
kentang	potatoes
kepiting	crab
kerang	mussels
kodok	frog

kuetiau	flat noodles
laksa	spicy noodle soup with coconut milk
lele	catfish
lontong	cubes of pressed rice often served with peanut sauce
martabak	• pancakes made with a choice of banana, chocolate, nuts, cheese and/ or condensed milk • savoury omelette in a thin pastry
mi/mie	noodles
mie goreng	fried noodles
mie kuah	noodlc soup
mie rebus	noodle soup
nasi ...	cooked rice ...
campur	with a selection of meat and vegetable dishes on one plate
goreng	fried
goreng istimewa/ spesial	fried with egg
kuning	cooked in turmeric and served with meat and vegetable side dishes
putih	boiled or steamed
rames	with a selection of meat and vegetable dishes on one plate
sayur	with vegetables
otak	brains
pangsit	soup with meat dumplings
pempek	fried sago dumpling with an egg inside (a Palembang speciality)
pete	large, tasty and odorous bean
pecel lele	fried catfish with chilli sauce
rendang	meat cooked slowly in spices and coconut
roti	bread
roti bakar	toast with jam and/or cheese

sate ...	satay (grilled meat on a stick served with peanut sauce)
ayam	chicken
daging	beef
kambing	goat
singkong	cassava/manioc (a root vegetable with edible leaves)
soto/sop	soup. Ingredients vary from region to region and take the name of the place of origin, such as **soto Madura, soto Bandung**

soto ayam	chicken soup
tahu	tofu
telur ...	... egg
ceplok	poached
goreng	fried
rebus	boiled
telur dadar	omelette
tempeh ...	... tempeh (fermented soybean)
goreng	fried
kering	dry fried
penyet	deep fried
tongseng	meat or chicken cooked in coconut milk
udang	shrimp
udang karang	lobster
ular	snake

Snacks & Sweets — Makanan Kecil dan Makanan manis

abon	spiced and shredded meat used as a filling or an accompaniment to rice dishes
agar	jelly made with seaweed
bala bala	vegetable fritter
biskit	small sweet biscuits in a multitude of shapes
dodol	chewy, toffee-like sweet (a Garot speciality)
emping	rice or tapioca crackers
es krim	ice cream (try durian flavour)
gorengan	fried snacks such as **pisang goreng**, **tahu isi** and **tempeh goreng**
kelepon	green rice balls with a palm sugar centre
kerupuk	prawn or rice crackers
ketan hitam	black sticky rice served with coconut milk
kue (lapis)	(layer) cake
kue sus	custard-filled pastry
lemper	sticky rice with **abon** filling wrapped in a banana leaf
lontong	cubes of pressed rice often served with peanut sauce
lumpia	soft spring rolls
manisan	sweets

BUNGKUS

Need to pack a picnic, or rations for a long haul? Nearly all restaurants and stalls can pack you food for the road. Even soup can be put in a bag for you. Just say:

Please put it in a container.	Minta bungkus.

nasi liwet	rice cooked in coconut milk with egg or chicken (a Solo speciality)
oncom	soybean cake
onde-onde	sesame balls with a green bean centre
perkedel	fried croquette with abon filling
pisang goreng	fried banana
pukis	crescent-shaped cake
putu	steamed cylindrical rice-flour cakes with a palm sugar centre
rujak	fruit salad in a sour, spicy sauce
tahu ...	tofu
isi	fried, with a vegetable filling
Sumedang	fried, from Sumedang. Why tofu from Sumedang tastes better is a mystery, but it does.
tiram	oysters

MIDNIGHT SNACK

For a late-night, post-clubbing feast, nothing beats a visit to a **lesehan** or a **warung gaul**.

A **lesehan** is a streetside eatery usually consisting of a few grass mats and a gas-burner to cook on. These places only appear after midnight, when footpaths are clear of merchandise and pedestrians. The lesehans in Yogyakarta can be great places to hang out, as locals, visitors and street kids share a mat and chat over a plate of **nasi goreng**, 'fried rice'.

A **warung gaul** is a portable cafe, recognised by the orange tarpaulin and kerosene lamp. The fare is simple – **teh**,'tea', **kopi**, 'coffee', **gorengan**, 'fried snacks' and **kue**, 'cakes'. Just eat what you want then tell the owner what you had at the end and the bill will be totalled. The **warung gaul** is the domain of **becak** drivers and local insomniacs, but a new face is always welcome.

MARKETS & SELF-CATERING / PASAR DAN MASAKAN SENDIRI

Whether you want to cook a meal yourself, stock up on fresh produce or compile a taste of home, your first stop has to be the pasar, 'market'.

This is the nucleus of any Indonesian town, holding the most intriguing array of local and imported produce. Although the greatest range of fruit is available in the wet season, there's always some fresh fruit on offer.

Apart from fresh produce, markets have a multitude of other goods on offer – rice and other grains, packaged goods, kitchenware, tobacco and so on. Your nose will know when you've hit the meat section.

Pasar swalayan, 'supermarkets' and toko umum, 'general stores' are convenient places to pick up extra supplies, and the larger businesses provide expats with imported tastes of home. At a price.

Can I please have ...?	Minta ...?
an orange	sebuah jeruk
a kilo of oranges	sekilo jeruk
two kilos of oranges	dua kilo jeruk
half a kilo of orange	setengah kilo jeruk
seven mangoes	tujuh mangga

How much is this?	Berapa harganya ini?
How much is a kilogram of ...?	Berapa harga sekilo ...?
Can I taste it?	Boleh coba?
I don't want that one.	Jangan yang itu.
Please give me another one.	Tolong kasih yang lain.

LIFE OF RICE

Rice in the field is called padi.
Rice grain at the market is called beras.
Cooked rice on your plate is nasi.

Staples — Makanan Pokok

bread	roti
noodles	mie
rice (cooked)	nasi

Fruit — Buah-buahan

apple	apel
avocado	alpukat/apokat (eaten as a dessert)
banana	pisang
cempedak	cempedak, similar to a jackfruit but sweeter, more tender
coconut	kelapa, look for kelapa muda, 'young coconut', which makes a refreshing drink
durian	durian, an encounter with this 'king of fruits' is a memorable experience for the fruit lover. Durians announce themselves in any market by exuding an incredibly pungent stench. If you can hold your breath long enough to approach, and swallow the rich, creamy flesh, you may get to crave the unique flavour.
guava	jambu, a hard, pear-shaped fruit. The small black seeds should not be eaten.
jackfruit	nangka. Sellers often break the fruit up into individual segments, which are then packed, ready to eat. The flesh is rubbery, sweet and strongly flavoured. Jackfruit trees are widely grown and can be recognised by their huge pendulous fruit, often wrapped in plastic bags for protection while they ripen on the tree.
lemon	jeruk nipis

mangosteen	manggis is easily recognised by its thick purple-brown fibrous skin, which protects the mouthwatering, sweet-sour white flesh inside
mango	mangga
orange	jeruk manis
pawpaw	papaya
peanuts	kacang
pineapple	nanas
rambutan	rambutan. Bright red fruit covered in soft, hairy spines, and containing a delicious, lychee-like, sweet white flesh
salak	salak, brown snake-skin fruit of the Zalacca palm, the flesh of which is crunchy and nutty
starfruit	belimbing, a watery thirst-quenching fruit shaped like a star when viewed end on. It's one of the few fruits eaten without being peeled or having their outer covering removed.
strawberry	arbei

EAT YOUR WORDS

While the word makan translates as 'to eat', it holds many other meanings – some not so appetising.

rumah makan	restaurant (lit: eating house)
makan pagi	breakfast (lit: morning feed)
makan tidur	to do nothing (lit: to-eat sleep)
makan waktu	to take a long time (lit: to-eat time)
makan uang	to take a bribe (lit: to-eat money)
makan angin	to get some fresh air (lit: to-eat wind)
makan tangan	to be hit in the face (lit: to-eat hand)
makan gaji	to earn a salary (lit: to-eat wage)

Vegetables — Sayur-Sayuran

beans	buncis
cabbage	kol
carrot	wortel
cauliflower	bunga kol
corn	jagung
cucumber	ketimun
eggplant	terong
mushrooms	jamur
onion	bawang bombay
potato	kentang
pumpkin	labu
tomato	tomat

CHILLI

cabe/lombok	chilli (the smaller the hotter)
pecel	spicy sauce made from chilli, peanuts and/or tomato
pedas	spicy
sambal	chilli sauce or paste

Meat — Daging

beef	daging sapi
brains	otak
chicken	ayam
duck	bebek
goat	kambing
heart	jantung
lamb	domba
liver	hati
mutton	domba
pig	babi
rabbit	kelinci

ROAST MY GOAT

baked	panggang
boiled	rebus
cooked in coconut milk	opor
fried	goreng
grilled	bakar
smoked	asap
spit-roasted	guling
steamed	kukus

Seafood — Makanan Laut

catfish	lele
crab	kepiting
freshwater fish	ikan tambak
lobster	udang karang
mussels	kerang
oysters	tiram
saltwater fish	ikan laut
shrimp	udang
squid	cumi-cumi

Spices & Condiments — Bumbu-bumbu

chilli	cabe
chilli sauce or paste	sambal
cinnamon	kayu manis
cloves	cengkeh
curry	kari
garlic	bawang putih
ginger	jahe
MSG (monosodium glutamate)	vetsin
oil	minyak
pepper	lada/merica
salt	garam

soy sauce (salty)	kecap asin
spicy sauce made from chilli, peanuts and/or tomato	pecel
sugar	gula
sweet soy sauce	kecap manis
tomato sauce	saus tomat
turmeric	kunyit
vinegar	cuka

DRINKS — MINUMAN

Many street vendors are dedicated to quenching the community's thirst. Drinks like es campur, 'mixed ice', are more of a dessert than a drink, and are often served in a bowl.

I want to drink ...	Saya mau minum ...
Do you have ...?	Ada ...?

SWEET, SWEET AVOCADO & CHEESE

Alpukat, 'avocados', are readily available throughout Indonesia, yet they often turn up in places you mightn't expect. Indonesians like to eat avocado as a dessert or sweet treat. Consequently, they form the basis of es alpukat, an avocado shake, made with chocolate syrup or condensed milk.

Keju, 'cheese', is also used in sweet snacks, such as roti bakar, a fried sandwich of cheese, jam and even chocolate sprinkles. There's even can be cheese icing on a kue, 'cake'.

Cold Drinks — Minuman Dingin

avocado blended with vanilla or chocolate syrup	**jus apokat**
black agar, 'seaweed' jelly with fruit syrup and ice	**es cincau**
citrus juice	**es jeruk**
coconut milk	**es kelapa muda**
coconut milk with fruit and ice	**es teler**
coconut milk with agar jelly and ice	**es cendol**
coconut milk with fruit, jelly and shaved ice	**es campur**
cordial	**sirup/stroop**
milk	**susu**
... water	**air ...**
bottled	**botol**
drinking	**putih**

Hot Drinks — Minuman Panas

Tea and coffee is nearly always served sweet. If you don't want sugar, ask for **teh/kopi pahit**, 'bitter tea/coffee'. Coffee is served black, sweet and chewy, and milk usually means condensed milk.

coffee ...	**kopi ...**
tea ...	**teh ...**
with sugar	**dengan gula**
without sugar	**pahit**
with milk	**dengan susu**
boiled water	**air matang**
ginger tea	**teh jahe**
strong ginger tea with coconut	**bandrek**

Alcohol / Minuman Keras

beer	bir
grape wine	anggur
palm tree spirits	tuak
rice wine	arak/brem
tapioca wine	brem

DI LUAR KOTA — IN THE COUNTRY

CAMPING — BERKEMAH

When camping or hiking in Indonesia, you'll discover that directions are often given in terms of compass points (see Getting Around, page 61).

Asking directions can prove problematic, as many people will say 'yes' out of politeness, even if they don't know the way. So if you ask 'Is the waterfall this way?', they may just agree. It would be better to ask: Air terjun dimana?, 'Where's the waterfall?' If in doubt, ask a few people.

Can we camp here?	Bisa berkemah di sini?
How much is it per person/tent?	Berapa harganya satu orang/tenda?
Where can I hire a tent?	Tenda disewa di mana?
Are there shower facilities?	Ada fasilitas mandi?

backpack	ransel
campground	tempat kemah
camping	berkemah
campsite	tempat tenda
firewood	kayu bakar
mat	tikar
mosquito net	kelambu
national park	taman nasional
penknife	pisau lipat
stove (burner)	kompor
tent	tenda
torch (flashlight)	senter

DID YOU KNOW ...

In southern Bali, utara, 'north', traditionally means 'toward the mountains'. In Yogyakarta, the looming Merapi Volcano *is* north, and locals use it to get their bearings.

HIKING — JALAN DI HUTAN

Are there any tourist attractions near here?	Ada tempat wisata dekat sini?
Where's the nearest village?	Di mana desa yang paling dekat?
Is it safe to climb this mountain?	Apakah aman mendaki gunung ini?
Is there a hut up there?	Apakah ada pondok di atas?
Do I need a guide?	Apakah saya perlu pemandu wisata?
Where can I find out about hiking trails in the region?	Di mana ada keterangan tentang jalan kecil di daerah ini?
I'd like to talk to someone who knows this area.	Saya mau bicara dengan seseorang yang tahu baik daerah ini.
How long is the trail?	Jarak jalanya berapa?
Is the track well marked?	Apakah jalanya mudah diikuti?
How high is the climb?	Berapa tinggi pendakian?
Which is the shortest/ easiest route?	Jalan yang mana paling cepat/mudah?
When does it get dark?	Mulai gelap jam berapa?
Is it very scenic?	Apakah pemandangannya indah?
Where can I hire mountain gear?	Alat mendaki gunung disewa di mana?
Where can we buy supplies?	Bahan makanan dijual di mana?

On the Path — Dalam Perjalanan

Where have you come from?	Anda baru dari mana?
How long did it take you?	Berapa lama dari sana?
Does this path go to ...?	Apakah jalan ini ke ...?
I'm lost.	Saya tersesat.
Where can we spend the night?	Bisa menginap di mana?
Can I leave some things here for a while?	Boleh simpan barang di sini sebentar?
There's a cave here.	Ada gua di sini.

altitude	ketinggian
binoculars	teropong
candles	lilin
to climb	mendaki/menaiki
compass	kompas
downhill	turun
first-aid kit	kotak pertolongan pertama
gloves	sarung tangan
guide	pemandu
guided trek	jalan yang dipandu
hiking	jalan di hutan
hiking boots	sepatu jalan
hunting	berburu
ledge	jurang
lookout	tempat meninjau
map	peta
mountain climbing	mendaki gunung
pick	beliung
provisions	perbekalan
rock climbing	panjat tebing
rope	tali/tambang
short cut	jalan potong
signpost	tanda
steep	curam
trek	perjalanan
uphill	naik
to walk	berjalan kaki

DON'T TRASH THE TEMPAT

Littering, sampah, is a problem in Indonesia's national parks. Sometimes it's impossible to get lost because of the trail of rubbish to follow.

Jangan buang sampah.	Don't litter.
Bawa pulang sampah sendiri.	Take your litter with you.

AT THE BEACH — DI PANTAI

Can we swim here?	Bisa berenang di sini?
Is it safe to swim here?	Aman berenang di sini?
What time is high/low tide?	Jam berapa pasang tinggi/ rendah?

coast	pantai
diving	menyelam
fishing	memancing
marine reserve	taman laut
reef	batu karang
sand	pasir
sea	laut
snorkelling	snorkel
sunblock	penahan matahari
sunglasses	kacamata hitam
surf	ombak
surfboard	papan selancar
surfing	berselancar
swimming	berenang
towel	handuk
waterski	ski air
waves	ombak
windsurfing	berselancar angin

Diving — Penyelaman

Are there good diving sites here?	Ada tempat penyelaman yang baik di sini?
Can we hire a diving boat/guide?	Apakah perahu/pemandu penyelaman bisa disewa?
We'd like to hire diving equipment.	Kami mau sewa alat penyelaman.
I'm interested in exploring wrecks.	Saya tertarik mencari kapal karam.

WEATHER — CUACA

Many Indonesians find it funny that westerners talk about the weather incessantly.

What's the weather like?	Bagaimana cuacanya?
Today it's ...	Hari ini ...
cloudy	mendung/berawan
cold	dingin
flooding	banjir
hot	panas
humid	lembab
raining heavily	hujan deras
raining lightly	gerimis
warm	hangat
wet	basah/hujan
windy	berangin
What time is ...?	Jam berapa matahari ...?
sunrise	terbit
sunset	terbenam
cloud	awan
fog	kabut
moon	bulan
mud	lumpur
rain	hujan

SEASONS

Indonesia has two seasons:

musim hujan	the rainy (monsoon) season, October to April
musim kemarau	the dry season, May to September

sky	langit
smoke	asap
storm	badai
sun	matahari (lit: eye of the day)
typhoon	topan

GEOGRAPHICAL TERMS — GEOGRAFI ISTILAH

atoll	atol
beach	pantai
bridge	jembatan
cave	gua/goa
city	kota
cliff	jurang
earth	bumi
earthquake	gempa bumi
estuary	muara
farm	kebun
footpath	jalan kecil
forest	hutan
gap (narrow pass)	puncak
harbour	pelabuhan
hill	bukit
hot spring	mata air panas
island	pulau
lake	danau
mountain (path)	(jalan) gunung
pass	puncak
peak	puncak
plain	dataran
river	sungai
rock	batu
sea	laut
valley	lembah
village	desa/kampung
volcano	gunung api
waterfall	air terjun

FAUNA — DUNIA BINATANG

FAUNA	DUNIA BINATANG
bird	burung
buffalo	kerbau
cat	kucing
chicken	ayam
cow	sapi
crocodile	buaya
dog	anjing
fish	ikan
frog	kodok
goat	kambing
horse	kuda
monkey	monyet
pig	babi
rooster	ayam jantan
sheep	domba
snake	ular
tiger	harimau

Insects — Serangga

ant	semut
butterfly	kupu-kupu
cockroach	kecoa
fly	lalat
leech	lintah
mosquito	nyamuk
spider	laba-laba

FLORA & AGRICULTURE — DUNIA TUMBUH-TUMBUHAN & PERTANIAN

agriculture	pertanian
cloves	cengkeh
coconut palm	pohon kelapa
corn	jagung
flower	bunga
fruit tree	pohon buah
to harvest	panen
irrigation	pengairan/irigasi
leaf	daun
to plant	menanam
rice field	sawah
rice terrace	petak sawah
sugar cane	tebu
tobacco	tembakau

With any luck, your time in Indonesia will be free of illness and you won't need to turn to this section at all. If you do need to talk about illness, the all-purpose word is sakit. As a verb, it means 'to feel sick' or 'to hurt', and when used as an adjective, it means 'sick' or 'painful'.

AT THE DOCTOR — DI DOKTER

Where's a ...	... di mana?
chemist (pharmacy)	apotik
dentist	dokter gigi
doctor	dokter
hospital	rumah sakit
regional clinic	puskesmas
I'm sick.	Saya sakit.
My friend is sick.	Teman saya sakit.
Is there a doctor here who speaks English?	Ada dokter yang berbahasa Inggris?
Could the doctor come to the hotel?	Apakah dokter bisa ke hotel?
I've had a blood test.	Darah saya sudah diperiksa.
I need a blood test.	Saya perlu periksa darah.
Is that a new syringe?	Apakah jarum suntik itu baru?
Please use this syringe.	Pakai jarum suntik ini.
I feel better/worse.	Saya merasa lebih baik/sakit.
This is my usual medicine.	Ini obat biasa saya.
I've been vaccinated.	Saya sudah divaksinasi.
I don't want a blood transfusion.	Saya tidak mau transfusi darah.
I need a receipt for my insurance.	Saya perlu kwitansi buat asuransi saya.

AILMENTS / PENYAKIT

I'm ill.	Saya sakit.
I feel under the weather.	Saya kurang enak badan.
I feel nauseous.	Saya mual.
I've been vomiting.	Saya muntah terus.
I can't sleep.	Saya tidak bisa tidur.

I feel ...	Saya merasa ....
dizzy	pusing
shivery	menggigil
weak	lemah

THEY MAY SAY ...

Anda hamil?	Are you pregnant?
Anda merasa sakit di mana?	Where does it hurt?
Anda punya alergi?	Are you allergic to anything?

Anda ...?	Do you ...?
merokok	smoke
minum minuman keras	drink
pakai obat bius	take drugs

Apakah anda demam/panas?	Do you have a temperature?
Apakah anda sedang menstruasi?	Are you menstruating?
Merasa sakit?	Do you feel any pain?
Pernah ada penyakit ini?	Have you had this before?
Sakit apa?	What's the matter?
Sedang pakai obat?	Are you on medication?
Sudah berapa lama merasabegini?	How long have you been like this?

My leg/foot is broken.	Kaki saya patah.
I have low/high blood. pressure.	Saya menderita tekanan darah rendah/tinggi.
My ... hurts	... saya sakit.
I'm suffering from (a/an) ...	Saya sakit ...
addiction	kecanduan
allergy	alergi
anaemia	anemi
asthma	asma
bite	gigitan
burns	luka bakar
cancer	kanker
cholera	kolera
cold	masuk angin; pilek
constipation	sukar buang air besar
cough	batuk
cystitis	kista
diarrhoea	diare/mencret
dog bite	gigitan anjing
dysentery	disentri
fever	demam
food poisoning	keracunan makanan
gastroenteritis	maag
headache	sakit kepala
heart condition	kondisi jantung
hepatitis	hepatitis
high blood pressure	tekanan darah tinggi
indigestion	salah cerna
infection	infeksi
influenza	selesma/pilek
itch	gatal
lice	kutu
malaria	malaria
migraine	sakit kepala berat
pain	sakit

rabies	rabies
rheumatism	encok
sore throat	sakit tenggorokan
sprain	keseleo
stomachache	sakit perut
sunburn	terbakar matahari
thrush	guam
travel sickness	mabuk/mual
typhoid	demam tipus
urinary tract infection	infeksi kencing
venereal disease	penyakit kelamin
worms	cacingan

WOMEN'S HEALTH — KESEHATAN WANITA

Is there a female doctor here?	Ada dokter wanita di sini?
Could I see a doctor for women?	Ada dokter khusus untuk wanita?
I'd like to use contraception.	Saya mencari kontrasepsi.
I haven't menstruated for ... weeks.	Saya belum mentruasi selama ... minggu.
I'm on the Pill.	Saya pakai pil kontrasepsi.
(I think) I'm pregnant.	(Mungkin) saya hamil.

abortion	aborsi
cystitis	kista
diaphragm	diafrakma
IUD	spiral
mamogram	mamogram
menstruation	menstruasi
miscarriage	keguguran
pap smear	tes kanker rahim

period pain — sakit menstruasi
the Pill — pil kontrasepsi
premenstrual tension — ketegangan sebelum menstruasi
thrush — guam
ultrasound — ultrasound

MASUK ANGIN

Whether you have the flu, a slight fever or are just feeling run-down, Indonesians will say **masuk angin**. This translates as 'the wind's got into you'.

SPECIAL HEALTH NEEDS — KEPERLUAN KHUSUS KESEHATAN

I'm ... — Saya sakit ...
- anaemic — anemia
- asthmatic — asma
- diabetic — kencing manis

I'm allergic to ... — Saya alergi ...
- antibiotics — antibiotika
- aspirin — aspirin
- bees — tawon
- codeine — kodein
- dairy products — makanan produk susu
- penicillin — penisilin
- pollen — serbuk sari

I have a skin allergy. — Kulit saya alergi.
I have my own syringe. — Saya punya jarum suntik sendiri.

I need a new pair of glasses. — Saya perlu kacamata baru.
I'm on medication for ... — Saya sedang pakai obat untuk ...

ALTERNATIVE TREATMENTS — PENGOBATAN ALTERNATIF

Although western-style medical treatment is the norm, alternative treatments – including some that are unique to Indonesia – are widely practised.

acupuncture	tusuk jarum
aromatherapy	pengobatan dengan aroma
faith healer	dukun
herbalist	ahli jamu
massage	pijit
meditation	meditasi
reflexology	refleksi
yoga	yoga

JAMU

If you're looking for alternative medicine, don't go past the toko jamu, 'herbal remedy shop'. There's a toko jamu in every town, easily identifiable by bright yellow decor and walls festooned with medicinal sachets. Choose your sachet according to the descriptive cheesy graphic, or ask the ahli jamu, 'herbalist', at the counter for assistance.

There are jamu remedies for everything – from bau badan, 'body odour' to lemah syahwat, 'impotence'. For the full jamu experience, ask the ahli jamu to whip up a remedy on the spot, complete with a raw egg yolk. It's enough to make you well.

You'll also find jamu sold on the street by sellers (usually women) who go from door to door with their jamu supplies in a basket on their back.

What jamu do you recommend for ...?	Anda menganjurkan jamu apa untuk ...?
Can you prepare it for me?	Bisa disiapkan?

FAITH HEALING

If you're feeling poorly, can't find a boyfriend, or you've lost your car keys, you should make a date with a **dukun**, 'a faith healer and mystic'. The **dukun** tradition is alive and well in Indonesia, although methods of treatment vary greatly between regions and even within the same area.

Generally speaking, there are two types of **dukun**. **Dukun putih**, 'white shaman' use such tools as **doa**, 'prayers'. **Dukun hitam**, 'black shaman' may use **roh**, 'spirits' and spells involving a symbolic **kris**, 'sword'.

People go to a **dukun** for many reasons, even to place a curse on an enemy.

PARTS OF THE BODY	BAGIAN TUBUH
ankle	pergelangan kaki
anus	dubur
appendix	usus buntu
arm	lengan
back	punggung
bladder	kandung kencing
blood	darah
bone	tulang
breast	buah dada
buttocks	pantat
chest	dada
chin	dagu
ear	telinga
eye	mata
face	wajah/muka
finger	jari tangan
foot	kaki

hands	tangan
head	kepala
heart	jantung
hip	pinggul
kidney	ginjal
knee	lutut
leg	kaki
liver	hati
lung	paru-paru
mouth	mulut
muscle	otot
neck	leher
nose	hidung
penis	zakar
ribs	tulang rusuk
shoulder	bahu/pundak
skin	kulit
stomach	perut
testicles	buah pelir
throat	tenggorokan
toes	jari kaki
tooth	gigi
vagina	vagina
vein	urat darah halus

THEY MAY SAY ...

Tablet-tablet ini harus diminum tiga kali sehari.	These tablets must be taken three times a day.
Kocok dulu sebelum diminum.	Shake the bottle before taking.

AT THE CHEMIST / DI APOTIK

I need medicine for ...	Saya perlu obat untuk ...
(Do) I need a prescription for ...(?)	(Apakah) saya perlu resep untuk ...(?)
How many times a day?	Berapa kali sehari?
antibiotics	antibiotik
antiseptic	antiseptik; penangkal infeksi
aspirin	aspirin
Band-aids	plaster
bandage	pembalut/perban
condoms	kondom
contraceptives	kontrasepsi
cotton wool	kapas
cough medicine	obat batuk
gauze	kabut tipis
headache tablets	obat sakit kepala
laxatives	obat cuci perut
painkillers	obat penawar sakit
penicillin	penisilin
prescription	resep
quinine	kina
rubbing alcohol	alkohol gosok
sleeping pills	pil tidur
tablet	tablet
vitamins	vitamin

Useful Words

accident	kecelakaan
breath	nafas
compress	kompres
disease	penyakit
faeces	kotoran/tinja
fast (n)	puasa
to fast	puasa
health	kesehatan

injection	jarum suntik
injury	luka
medicine	obat
oxygen	oksigen
poisonous	beracun
urine	air seni
wound	luka

AT THE DENTIST — DI DOKTER GIGI

I have a toothache.	Saya sakit gigi.
I have a cavity.	Ada lubang.
My tooth is broken.	Gigi saya patah.
I've lost a filling.	Tambalan gigi saya hilang.
My gums hurt.	Gusi saya sakit.
I don't want it extracted.	Jangan cabut.
Please give me an anaesthetic.	Tolong kasih obat bius.
Ouch!	Aduh!

KEPERLUAN KHUSUS

SPECIFIC NEEDS

DISABLED TRAVELLERS — ORANG CACAT

I'm disabled/handicapped.	Saya cacat.
I need assistance.	Saya perlu dibantu.
What services do you have for disabled people?	Ada pelayanan untuk orang cacat?
Is there wheelchair access?	Ada jalan masuk untuk kursi roda?
I'm deaf. Speak more loudly please.	Saya tuli. Tolong bicara lebih keras.
I can lipread.	Saya dapat membaca gerak bibir.
I have a hearing aid.	Saya punya alat bantu dengar.
Does anyone here know ... sign language?	Ada orang yang bisa berbahasa isyarat ...?
Are guide dogs permitted?	Apakah anjing penuntun bisa masuk?

braille library	perpustakaan orang tuna netra
disabled person	orang cacat
guide dog	anjing penuntun
wheelchair	kursi roda

GAY TRAVELLERS — ORANG GAY

There are lively gay scenes in Indonesia's larger towns and tourist areas. Generally speaking, Indonesians are fairly accepting of homosexual couples.

Where are the gay hangouts?	Di mana tempat kumpul orang gay?
Where are the gay clubs?	Orang gay pergi ke klub malam mana?
Is there a gay street/district?	Ada jalan/daerah gay di kota ini?

Are we/Am I likely to be harassed? — Apakah orang gay sering diganggu di sini?
Is there a gay organisation in Surabaya city? — Apakah ada organisasi gay di kota Surabaya?

SHE-MALES

Indonesia has a very active transvestite and transsexual scene. In Indonesia, transsexuals and transvesties are known as **banci**, or **waria**, a word derived from **wanita**,'woman' and **pria**, 'man'.

TRAVELLING WITH THE FAMILY — PERJALANAN KELUARGA

Are there facilities for babies? — Apakah ada fasilitas untuk bayi?
Do you have a childminding service? — Apakah ada servis penjagaan anak?
Where can I find a (English-speaking) babysitter? — Penjaga anak (yang bicara dalam Bahasa Inggeris) bisa dicari di mana?
Can you put an (extra) bed/cot in the room? — Bisa minta satu tempat tidur/pelbet (lagi) di kamar?
I need a car with a child seat. — Saya perlu mobil dengan kursi anak.
Is it suitable for children? — Apakah ini cocok untuk anak?
Are there any activities for children? — Apakah ada kegiatan untuk anak?
Is there a family discount? — Ada diskon untuk keluarga?
Are children allowed? — Apakah anak bisa masuk?
Do you have a children's menu? — Apakah ada daftar makanan untuk anak?

LOOKING FOR A JOB — MENCARI PEKERJAAN

Where can I find local job advertisements?	Pekerjaan diiklankan di mana?
Do I need a work permit?	Apakah saya perlu visa kerja?
I've had experience.	Saya sudah berpengalaman.
I've come ...	Saya datang ...
I'm ringing ...	Saya telpon ...
about the position advertised.	mengenai jabatan yang diiklankan.
What is the salary?	Gajinya berapa?
Do I have to pay tax?	Harus bayar pajak?

I can start ...	Saya bisa mulai ...
today	hari ini
tomorrow	besok
next week	minggu depan
casual	kerja tidak tetap
employee	pekerja/karyawan
employer	majikan
full-time	penuh waktu
job	pekerjaan
occupation	pekerjaan
part-time	paruh waktu
resume	riwayat hidup
trade	pekerjaan
traineeship	kedudukan sebagai siswa latihan

ON BUSINESS — PERJALANAN BISNIS

We're attending a ...	Kami menghadiri ...
conference	konferensi
meeting	pertemuan/rapat
trade fair	pekan raya dagang
I'm on a course.	Saya sedang kursus.
I have an appointment with ...	Saya ada janji dengan ...
Here's my business card.	Ini kartu nama saya.
I need an interpreter.	Saya perlu penerjemah.
I'd like to use a computer.	Saya perlu pakai komputer.
I'd like to send a fax/an email.	Saya mau mengirim fax/email.
client	langganan/klien
colleague	rekan
distributor	penyalur
email	email
exhibition	pameran
manager	menejer/pemimpin
mobile phone	ponsel; telpon genggam
profit	untung
proposal	usul

ON TOUR — PERJALANAN WISATA

We're part of a group.	Kami dalam kelompok.
We're on tour.	Kami sedang berkeliling.
I'm with the ...	Saya dengan ...
band	kaum
crew	awak
group	kelompok
team	regu
Please speak with our manager.	Bicaralah dengan pemimpin/ menejer kami.
We've lost our equipment.	Peralatan kami hilang.

We sent equipment on this ...	Peralatan kami dikirimkan dengan ... ini.
bus	bis
flight	pesawat
train	kereta
We're taking a break of ... days.	Kami beristirahat selama ... hari.
We're performing on (date) ...	Kami bermain pada tanggal ...

FILM & TV CREWS — KRU FILEM & TELEVISI

Can we film here?	Boleh filem di sini?
We're filming!	Kami sedang membuat filem!
We're making a ...	Kami membuat ....
film	filem
documentary	filem dokumentasi
TV series	sinetron

PILGRIMAGE & RELIGION — NAIK HAJI & KEAGAMAAN

Can I attend this service/mass?	Boleh mengikuti misa ini?
Can I pray here?	Boleh berdoa di sini?
Where can I pray/worship?	Tempat berdoa di mana?
Where can I make confession (in English)?	Pengakuan (dalam Bahasa Inggris) dilakukan di mana?
Can I receive communion here?	Bisa terima komuni di sini?

WHO'S WHO

balian	female shaman of the Tanjung Dayak people of Kalimantan
muezzin	people who call the faithful to the mosque
pedanda	high priest
pemangku	temple priest
santri	orthodox, devout Muslim

baptism	pembaptisan
christening	pembaptisan
church	gereja
communion	komuni suci
confession	pengakuan
funeral	pemakaman
God	Tuhan; Allah (Muslim)
monk	rahib
prayer	doa
priest (Catholic)	romo/pastor
priest (Protestant)	pendeta
relic	peninggalan
religious procession	arak-arakan agama
sabbath	Hari Sabat
saint	santo; orang suci
shrine	tempat suci
... temple	
Buddhist	candi
Chinese	kelenteng
Hindu	pura

TRACING ROOTS & HISTORY

MENCARI LELUHUR & SEJARAH

I think my ancestors came from this area.	**Saya kira leluhur saya berasal dari daerah ini.**
I'm looking for my relatives.	**Saya mencari keluarga saya.**
I have/had a relative who lives around here.	**Dulu keluarga saya tinggal di daerah ini.**
Is there anyone here by the name of ...?	**Apakah ada orang di sini bernama ...?**
I'd like to go to the cemetery/ burial ground.	**Saya ingin ke kuburan.**

HAJ

With a pilgrimage to Mecca being one of the tenets of the Islamic faith, thousands of Indonesian Muslims make the journey to Saudi Arabia at least once in their lives. Travel to Mecca is subsidised by the Indonesian government, and many villages raise their funds collectively and make the journey together.

calon haji	intending pilgrims
haj	pilgrimage (to Mecca)
haji (m)/haja (f)	pilgrim
naik haji	to go on a pilgrimage
ONH (ongkos naik haji)	government set price to go on a pilgrimage (set annually by the Department of Religious Affairs)
Tanah Suci	Holy Land

GODS & MYTHOLOGY

Barong	mythical lion-dog creature
Bodhisattva	divine being worthy of nirvana who remains on earth to offer guidance
Brahma	'the creator', a chief Hindu god
Dewi Sri	rice goddess
Garuda	mythical man-bird, the vehicle of Vishnu and the symbol of Indonesia
marapu	Sumbanese term for all spiritual forces such as gods, spirits & ancestors
naga	mythical snake-like creature
Rangda	evil black-magic spirit of Balinese tales and dances
Sanghyang Widi	Balinese supreme being, but in practice one of the lesser gods
Shiva	'the destroyer', a chief Hindu god
Vishnu	'the sustainer', a chief Hindu god
wali songo	the 'nine holy men' who propagated Islam in Java

JAM, TANGGAL & PERAYAAN — TIME, DATES & FESTIVALS

If you make an arrangement to meet someone, don't be alarmed if they turn up late. It's said that Indonesians often work on jam karet, 'rubber time'.

TELLING THE TIME — JAM BERAPA

In Indonesian 'am' and 'pm' are replaced by whole words rather than abbreviations.

8 am	jam delapan pagi (lit: hour eight in-the-morning)
8 pm	jam delapan malam (lit: hour eight at-night)

o'clock	jam (lit: hour)
second	detik
minute	menit
past	lewat/lebih (lit: plus)
to	kurang (lit: minus)
half	setengah
quarter	seperempat
one hour	satu jam
two hours	dua jam

What time is it?	Jam berapa (sekarang)? (lit: hour how-much (now)?)
It's three o'clock.	Jam tiga. (lit: hour three)
It's a quarter to four.	Jam empat kurang seperempat. (lit: hour four minus quarter)
It's ten past three.	Jam tiga lewat sepuluh. (lit: hour three plus ten)

Unlike English, 'five thirty' isn't given as 'half past five' but, as in German and Dutch, 'half to six'.

It's five-thirty.	**Jam setengah enam.** (lit: hour half six)
Half past one.	**Setengah dua.** (lit: half two)

Similarily, nights are often referred to in reference to the following day. 'Saturday night' is often expressed as 'the night before Sunday', rather like saying 'Christmas Eve'.

Saturday night	**malam Minggu** (lit: at-night Sunday)

However, the following construction is also understood:

Saturday night	**hari Sabtu malam** (lit: day Saturday at-night)

in the morning (1 – 11 am)	**pagi**
in the afternoon (11 am – 3 pm)	**siang**
in the evening (3 – 6 pm)	**sore**
at night (6 – 12 pm)	**malam**

DAYS — HARI DALAM SEMINGGU

DAYS	HARI DALAM SEMINGGU
Monday	**hari Senin**
Tuesday	**hari Selasa**
Wednesday	**hari Rabu**
Thursday	**hari Kamis**
Friday	**hari Jumat**
Saturday	**hari Sabtu**
Sunday	**hari Minggu**

On Monday. — **Pada hari Senin.**

MONTHS / BULAN

January	Januari
February	Februari
March	Maret
April	April
May	Mei
June	Juni

July	Juli
August	Agustus
September	September
October	Oktober
November	November
December	Desember

During June. — Selama bulan Juni.

MELTING MOMENTS

moment	sebentar
minute	menit
hour	jam
day	hari
week	minggu
fortnight	dua minggu
month	bulan
year	tahun
decade	dasawarsa
century	abad
millennium	masa seribu tahun

DATES — TANGGAL

The number of the day precedes the name of the month in Indonesian dates.

> 17 August 1945
> tujuh belas Agustus sembilan belas empat-puluh lima
> (lit: 17 August nineteen four-ten five)

What date is it today?	Tanggal berapa hari ini? (lit: date how-much day this?)
It's 28 June.	Tanggal dua-puluh delapan Juni. (lit: date two-ten eight June)
It's 1 April.	Tanggal satu April. (lit: date one April)

WHERE WERE YOU IN ...?

the 70s	tujuh puluhan
the 80s	delapan puluhan
the 90s	sembilan puluhan

PRESENT — SEKARANG

immediately	sekarang ini
now	sekarang
currently	sedang
today	hari ini
this morning	pagi ini
during the day	siang ini
tonight	malam ini/nanti malam
this week	minggu ini
this month	bulan ini
this year	tahun ini

PAST — YANG LALU

just now	baru saja
before	sebelum
recently	baru-baru ini
already	sudah
yesterday	kemarin
yesterday morning	kemarin pagi
yesterday afternoon	kemarin siang

last night	tadi malam, kemarin malam
day before yesterday	kemarin dulu
last week	minggu lalu
two weeks ago	dua minggu yang lalu
last month	bulan lalu
last year	tahun lalu
ago	yang lalu
a while ago	beberapa waktu yang lalu
long ago	dahulu

SEASONS

spring	musim semi/bunga
summer	musim panas
autumn	musim gugur
winter	musim dingin
dry season	musim kemarau/kering
rainy season	musim hujan

FUTURE — MASA DEPAN

as soon as possible	secepat mungkin
soon	segera
not yet	belum
later	nanti
after	sesudah
tomorrow	besok
tomorrow morning	besok pagi
tomorrow afternoon	besok siang
tomorrow evening	besok sore
day after tomorrow	lusa
next week	minggu depan
next month	bulan depan
next year	tahun depan
forever	selamanya

TOMMOROW NEVER COMES

Indonesians often use the words **besok** and **kemarin**, 'tomorrow' and 'yesterday' when talking broadly about the past and the future. So if someone says **kemarin saya sakit**, 'yesterday I was sick', it may not necessarily have been one day ago.

DURING THE DAY — SEPANJANG HARI

dawn	pagi buta/pagi-pagi
day	hari
early	lebih awal
early morning	pagi pagi benar
midday	tengah hari
midnight	tengah malam
sunrise	matahari terbit
sunset	matahari terbenam

HOLIDAYS & FESTIVALS

LIBURAN & PERAYAAN

There are many religious dates observed and celebrated by Indonesia's various communities.

Hari Proklamasi Kemerdekaan

Indonesia's Independence Day, falls on August 17 and is marked with a national holiday. The speeches, marches and flag waving in Jakarta are broadcast across the country.

Idul Adha

This Muslim festival commemorates Ibrahim's devotion to God. On being ordered by God to kill his son, Isaac, Ibrahim was about to do the deed when God put a stop to it and told him to kill a sheep instead.

The sacrifice – of a goat or a sheep – is repeated en masse throughout Muslim areas of Indonesia on **Idul Adha** and, once again, feasting ensues.

Lebaran

The first day of the 10th month marks the end of **Ramadan** and the celebration of **Lebaran** – also known as **Idul Fitri**.

Lebaran begins with mass prayers at mosques and in city squares, followed by two days of family visits and culinary engorgement. It's a time when children ask forgiveness from their parents for any wrongdoings, using the words **mohon ma'af lahir batin**, 'I apologise with my heart and soul'.

Travel before and during **Lebaran** can be difficult, as the whole country endeavours to get home for celebrations. Flights will be full, trains will be packed and traffic will be jammed.

Nyepi

Nyepi, the end of the Balinese lunar calendar, falls in March/April. The day before Nyepi, evil spirits are chased away with much noise and mayhem. On Nyepi people stay indoors and shops are shut. Consequently the evil spirits look around, find nothing to play mischief with, and leave.

Ramadan

The ninth month of the Muslim calendar is the month of Ramadan, also known as **bulan puasa**, 'the fasting month'. During Ramadan, many Muslims abstain from drinking, eating, smoking, sex and other pleasures during daylight hours. The fast is symbolic of a person's faith, and is also a way for Muslims to feel an affinity for those who are too poor to afford food.

Children, pregnant or menstruating women, the ill and the elderly aren't expected to fast. However some women 'make up' for missed fasting days later in the year.

No one is forced to fast, but it's polite to be discreet and eat indoors only. Many restaurants and food stalls remain open, with a shade cloth over the door.

At the end of the fasting month, travel can be hard to organise, as Muslims head for home to celebrate Lebaran with their families.

Other national holidays include:

Hari Natal
   Christmas, the birthday of Jesus Christ (December 25)

Isra Miraj Nabi Muhammed
   the ascension of the prophet Mohammed

Jumat Besar
   Good Friday (April)

Maulud Nabi Muhammed
the birthday of the prophet Mohammed (June)

Muharram
Islamic New Year

Paskah
Easter (April)

Waisak Day
marks the birth, enlightenment and death of Buddha (between May and June)

BIRTHDAY MIRTH!

Birthdays aren't a big deal once people are out of school. If you want to make it a big deal, here are the lyrics you need. The tune is different too, as it's based on the Dutch version.

Panjang umurnya	Live long
Panjang umurnya	Live long
Panjang umurnya serta mulia	Live long and glorious
Serta mulia	As well as glorious
Serta mulia	As well as glorious
Selamat Hari Ulang Tahun!	Happy Birthday!
Panjang umurnya!	Long life!
hari ulang tahun (lit: day repeat year)	birthday

WEDDINGS — PERNIKAHAN

Weddings are big business in Indonesia. Depending on the faith and/or wealth of the family, weddings can last for days. It's not uncommon to be invited to a wedding, even if you've never met the marrying couple.

Although offering gifts is acceptable, it's customary to give money in an envelope. Usually there's a box at the entrance for this purpose.

Congratulations!	**Semoga bahagia!**
wedding	**pernikahan/perkawinan**

FUNERALS — PEMAKAMAN

As with weddings, funerals can be gargantuan ceremonies. The funerals of Central Sulawesi and Sumba often involve the slaughter of many animals, and end up costing the bereaved family a fortune. Funerals can be very public affairs, and you may well be invited to attend one.

My condolences.	**Kami ikut berduka cita.**

BILANGAN & JUMLAH — NUMBERS & AMOUNTS

In Indonesian, numbers from 11 to 19 are comprised of the numbers one to nine plus the suffix **-belas**. Numbers from 20 to 99 are counted with the suffix '10', **-puluh**. **Sepuluh** is 10, **dua-puluh** is 20 and so on.

In the hundreds, the suffix **-ratus** is used. So, **seratus** is 100, **dua-ratus** is 200, and so on. The suffix for thousands is **-ribu**, and **-juta** is the suffix for millions.

CARDINAL NUMBERS — BILANGAN POKOK

0	nol
1	satu
2	dua
3	tiga
4	empat
5	lima
6	enam
7	tujuh
8	delapan
9	sembilan
10	sepuluh
11	sebelas
12	dua belas
13	tiga belas
14	empat belas
15	lima belas
16	enam belas
17	tujuh belas
18	delapan belas
19	sembilan belas
20	dua puluh
21	dua puluh satu
22	dua puluh dua
30	tiga puluh

40	empat-puluh
50	lima-puluh
100	seratus
200	dua-ratus
268	dua-ratus enam-puluh delapan
300	tiga-ratus
1000	seribu
2000	dua-ribu
3000	tiga-ribu
51,783	lima-puluh-satu-ribu, tujuh-ratus delapan-puluh tiga
1 million	sejuta
2 million	dua-juta

ORDINAL NUMBERS — BILANGAN TINGKAT

1st	pertama
2nd	kedua
3rd	ketiga
4th	keempat
5th	kelima
6th	keenam
7th	ketujuh
8th	kedelapan
9th	kesembilan
10th	kesepuluh

the first bus	bis (yang) pertama
the third building	gedung (yang) ketiga

HUNDREDS & THOUSANDS

To form the expression such as 'hundreds', just add -an to the suffix for hundred, thousand or million, and drop the se- syllable.

hundreds of people	ratusan orang
thousands of dollars	ribuan dolar
millions of ants	jutaan semut

FRACTIONS PECAHAN

1/3	sepertiga
1/4	seperempat
1/2	setengah
3/4	tiga perempat

QUANTITY JUMLAH

Quantity can either be indicated by a number, or by a quantity word placed before a noun.

all	semua
both	keduanya/dua-duanya
double	dobel
each	tiap-tiap/setiap
enough	cukup
every	masing-masing
few	beberapa
a little	sedikit
many	banyak
much	banyak
one more	satu lagi
some	beberapa

There are many people. Ada banyak orang.
(lit: there-are many person)

about	kira-kira
amount	jumlah
to count	menghitung
dozen	lusin
minus	kurang
more	lebih
number	nomor/angka/bilangan
a pair	sepasang
percent	persen
plus	tambah
quantity	jumlah
some	beberapa

DARURAT — EMERGENCIES

Help!	Tolong!
Stop!	Stop!
Go away!	Pergi!
Watch out!	Awas!
Thief!	Maling!
Pickpocket!	Copet!
Fire!	Kebakaran!
It's an emergency!	Darurat!
There's been an accident.	Ada kecelakaan.
Help me please!	Minta tolong!
Could I use the telephone?	Bisa pakai telepon?
I'm lost.	Saya tersesat.
Where are the toilets?	WC di mana?
Call the police!	Panggil polisi!
I'll get the police!	Saya panggil polisi!
Where's the police station?	Kantor polisi di mana?
I've been robbed!	Saya dirampok!
I speak English.	Saya berbahasa Inggris.

I've lost my ...	... saya hilang.
My ... was/were stolen.	... saya dicuri.
backpack	Ransel
bags	Tas
handbag	Tas tangan
money	Uang
papers	Dokumen
passport	Paspor
travellers cheques	Cek turis/perjalanan
wallet	Dompet

DEALING WITH THE POLICE / BERURUSAN DENGAN POLISI

My possessions are insured.	Barang saya diasuransi.
What am I accused of?	Saya dituduh apa?
I (don't) understand.	Saya (tidak) mengerti.
I didn't realise I was doing anything wrong.	Saya tidak tahu saya bersalah.
I didn't do it.	Saya tidak melakukan itu.

THE POLICE MAY SAY ...

Anda dituduh melakukan ...	You'll be charged with ...
Dia dituduh melakukan ...	S/he'll be charged with ...
bekerja tanpa izin	working without a permit
kegiatan subversif	anti-government activity
masuk tanpa izin	illegal entry
masuk tanpa visa	entry without a visa
mengganggu keamanan	disturbing the peace
memiliki barang tidak sah	possession of illegal substances
pelanggaran lalu-lintas	traffic violation
pembunuhan	murder
pencurian	theft
pencurian di toko	shoplifting
perampokan	robbery
perkosaan	rape
serangan	assault
tinggal terus sesudah visa habis	overstaying your visa

I'm sorry. I apologise.	Saya menyesal. Saya minta maaf.
We're innocent.	Kami tidak bersalah.
We're foreigners.	Kami orang asing.
Can I call someone?	Boleh telpon seseorang?
Can I see a lawyer who speaks English?	Minta advokat yang berbahasa Inggris.
Is there a fine we can pay to clear this?	Apakah kami bisa bayar denda supaya masalah ini selesai?
Can we pay an on-the-spot fine?	Bisa bayar denda sekarang?
I know my rights.	Saya tahu hak saya.
I want to contact my embassy/consulate.	Saya mau menghubungi kedutaan besar/konsulat saya.

arrested	ditangkap
cell	sel
consulate	konsulat
embassy	kedutaan besar
fine	denda
(not) guilty	(tidak) bersalah
lawyer	advokat
police officer	polisi
police station	kantor polisi
prison	penjara
trial	pengadilan

HEALTH / KESEHATAN

I'm ill.	Saya sakit.
My friend is ill.	Teman saya sakit.
Call an ambulance!	Panggil ambulans!
Call a doctor!	Panggil dokter!
Please take me/us to a hospital.	Tolong antar saya/kami ke rumah sakit.
My blood group is (A, B, O, AB) positive/negative.	Golongan darah saya (A, B, O, AB) positif/negatif.

EMERGENCIES

My contact number is ...	Nomor telepon saya ...
The number of my next of kin. is ...	Nomor telepon keluarga saya ...
I have medical insurance.	Saya punya asuransi kesehatan.
Please get medicine from the chemist for me.	Tolong beli obat untuk saya di apotik.

Root words (see Grammar, page 19) are given in brackets after verbs. (Root words are often used in place of active verbs by Indonesian speakers.)

to look	melihat [lihat]

Remember that nouns don't change their form according to whether they're singular or plural.

In this dictionary, when there is a choice between two words, they are separated by slashes:

afternoon	siang/sore
airport	lapangan udara/terbang

A

to be able (can) bisa/boleh

Can (may) I take your photo?
Boleh ambil foto anda?
Can you show me (on the map)?
Tolong tunjukkan (di peta)?

aboard	di atas
abortion	aborsi
above	di atas
abbreviation	singkatan
abroad	luar negri
to accept	menerima [terima]
accident	kecelakaan
accommodation	penginapan/akomodasi
to accompany	menemani
to acknowledge	mengakui
across	seberang
activist	aktivis
actually	sebenarnya
adaptor (electric)	pencocok
addiction	kecanduan
address (of house)	alamat
to admire	mengagumi [kagum]
admission (entry)	izin masuk
adult	dewasa
advice	nasehat
aerogram	aerogram
aeroplane	pesawat terbang • udara
afraid	takut

to be afraid of
takut [takut]

after	sesudah/setelah
afternoon	siang/sore

A

DICTIONARY

in the afternoon
pada siang/sore

this afternoon	nanti siang/sore
again	lagi
against (opposed)	melawan
age	umur
agent	agen
aggressive	agresif
ago	yang lalu

(half an hour) ago
(setengah jam) yang lalu
(three days) ago
(tiga hari) yang lalu

to agree	setuju [setuju]

I don't agree.
Saya tidak setuju.
Agreed.
Setuju.

agriculture	pertanian
ahead	di depan

straight ahead
terus

aid (help)	tolong/bantu
AIDS	AIDS
air	udara
air-conditioned	AC (pronounced *ah-che*)
airmail	pos udara
airport	bandara • lapangan udara/terbang
airport tax	pajak bandara
alarm clock	jam weker
alive	hidup
all	semua
allergic	alergi
allergy	alergi
alley	gang
to allow	membolehkan [boleh]

It's (not) allowed.
(Tidak) boleh.

almost	hampir
alone	sendirian
already	sudah
also	juga
altitude	ketinggian
always	selalu
amateur	amatir
ambassador	duta besar
among	di antara
anarchist	anarki
ancient	kuno
and	dan
angry	marah
animal	binatang
to annoy	mengganggu [ganggu]
to answer	menjawab [jawab]
ant	semut
antibiotics	antibiotik
antiques	barang antik
antiseptic	penangkal infeksi
any	apa saja
anything	apa saja
anytime	kapan saja
anywhere	di mana saja

apple	apel
appointment	janji
appropriate	cocok
approximately	kira-kira
archaeological	kepurbakalaan
architect	arsitek
architecture	arsitektur
to argue	membantah [bantah]
arm (of body)	lengan
to arrive	datang [datang] • tiba [tiba]
arrivals	kedatangan
art	seni
artist	seniman
artwork	karya seni
ashamed	malu
ashtray	asbak
to ask	
(for something)	minta [minta]
(a question)	bertanya [tanya]
asleep	tidur
aspirin	obat sakit kepala
assault	serangan
assist	membantu [bantu]
assistance	bantuan
asthma	asma
at	
(location)	di
(time)	pada
ATM (automatic teller machine)	ATM (anjungan tunai mandiri)
atmosphere	
(of planet)	atmosfir
(of place)	suasana
aunt	bibi/tante
automatic teller machine (ATM)	anjungan tunai mandiri (ATM)
autumn	musim gugur
avenue	jalan raya
avocado	alpukat/apokat

B

baby	bayi
baby food	makanan untuk bayi
baby powder	bedak bayi
babysitter	penjaga anak
back (of body)	punggung
at the back (behind)	di belakang
backpack	ransel
bad	
(attitude)	jahat
(weather)	buruk
(thought)	jelek
bag	tas
baggage	barang-barang • bagasi
baggage claim	pengambilan barang
bakery	toko roti
balcony	balkon
ball (for sport)	bola
ballet	balet
ballpoint pen	bolpoin
banana	pisang
band (music)	band
bandage	pembalut/perban
bank	bank
bank clerk	pegawai bank
bankdraft	surat wesel

banknote kontan/duit
baptism pembaptisan
bar (drinks) bar
barber tukang cukur rambut
to bargain tawar-menawar [tawar]
basket keranjang
bath mandi
to bathe mandi [mandi]
bathing suit baju renang
bathroom kamar mandi
battery aki/baterai
to be (see Grammar, page 33)
beach pantai
bean buncis
beautiful
(scenery) indah
(thing) bagus
(woman) cantik
because karena/sebab
bed tempat tidur
bedroom kamar tidur
beef daging sapi
beer bir
before sebelum
beggar orang minta-minta • orang jalanan
begin mulai
behind di belakang
below di bawah
beside di samping
best terbaik • paling baik
a bet taruhan
better lebih baik
between antara
the Bible Kitab/Injil
bicycle sepeda
big besar
bike sepeda
bill
(note) kontan/duit
(account) bon/rekening
binoculars teropong
biography biografi
bird burung
birth certificate surat lahir
birthday hari ulang tahun
birthday cake kue hari ulang tahun
to bite menggigit [gigit]
bite (dog/insect) gigitan
black hitam
B&W (film) (filem) hitam putih
blanket selimut
to bleed berdarah [darah]
blind (no vision) buta
blood darah
blood group golongan darah
blood pressure tekanan darah
blood test periksa darah
blue biru
a board papan
to board (ship, etc) naik [naik]
boarding pass pas naik
boat perahu
body badan
boil rebus
boiled egg telur rebus

boiled water	air matang
bone	tulang
book	buku
to make a booking	memesan [pesan]
bookshop	toko buku
boots	sepatu tinggi
border	perbatasan
bored	bosan
boring	membosankan
to borrow	meminjam [pinjam]
both	keduanya • dua-duanya
Don't bother.	Jangan repot.
bottle	botol
bottle opener	alat pembuka botol
(at the) bottom	di bawah
box (package)	kotak
boxing (sport)	tinju
boy	anak (laki-laki)
boyfriend	pacar (laki-laki)
brain	otak
branch (of office)	cabang
brave	berani
bread	roti
break (fracture)	pecah
breakfast	makan pagi
breath	napas
to bribe	menyogok [sogok]
bridge	jembatan
brilliant	bagus
to bring	membawa [bawa]
broken	patah
broom	sapu
... brother	... laki-laki
older	kakak
younger	adik
brown	coklat
a bruise	luka memar
bucket	ember
Buddhist	penganut Buda
bug (insectl)	hama/ serangga
to build	membangun [bangun]
building	gedung
burn	bakar
... bus	bis ...
city	kota
intercity	antar kota
bus station	stasiun • terminal bis
bus stop	stopan bis
business	perusahaan/ bisnis
businessperson	pengusaha
busker	pemain musik jalanan
busy	
(place/party)	ramai
(time)	sibuk
but	tetapi
butter	mentega
butterfly	kupu-kupu
buttons	kancing
to buy	membeli [beli]

C

cabbage	kol
cabin	ruang
cake	kue
calm	tenang
camera	kamera
camera operator	petugas kamera
camera shop	toko kamera
to camp	berkemah [kemah]
can (able)	bisa/boleh

Can we camp here?
Bisa berkemah di sini?

campsite	tempat tenda
can (aluminium)	kaleng
to cancel	membatalkan [batal]
candle	lilin
can opener	alat pembuka kaleng
car	mobil
carpark	tempat parkir
car registration	pendaftaran mobil
card (name)	kartu nama
cards (playing)	kartu (main)
careful	hati-hati
caring	pemeliharaan
to carry	membawa [bawa]
carton	karton
cartoons	kartun
cash	duit/kontan
cash register	mesin kas
cashier	kasir/kassa
cassette	kaset
castle	benteng/istana
cat	kucing
cathedral	katedral
Catholic	Katolik
cave	gua/goa
CD	CD (pronounced ***see-dee***)
to celebrate	merayakan [raya]
centimetre	sentimeter
ceramic	keramik
certificate	surat keterangan
chair	kursi
champagne	sampanye
championships	kejuaraan
chance	kesempatan/ kemungkinan
to change	mengganti [ganti]
changing rooms	kamar ganti pakaian
charming	luwes
to chat up	bercumbu-cumbuan [cumbu]
cheap	murah

Cheat!
Penipu!

to check	memeriksa [periksa]
check-in (desk)	tempat mend-aftarkan diri

Checkmate!
Sekakmat!

checkpoint	pos pemeriksaan

Cheers!
Selamat!

cheese	keju
chemist (pharmacy)	apotik
cheque	cek
chess	catur
chess board	papan catur
chest (of body)	dada
chewing gum	permen karet
chicken	ayam
child	anak
childminding	penjagaan anak
children	anak-anak
chilli	cabe
chocolate	coklat
cholera	kolera
to choose	memilih [pilih]
Christian	Kristen
Christmas Day	Hari Natal
Christmas Eve	Malam Natal
church	gereja
cigarette (papers)	(kertas) rokok
clove cigarettes	kretek
cinema	bioskop
circus	sirkus
citizenship	kewarganegaraan
city	kota
city walls	tembok kota
civil rights	hak asasi manusia (HAM)
class	kelas

1st class
kelas satu • eksekutif

2nd class
kelas dua/bisnis

class system	sistem golongan
classical art	seni klasik
classical theatre	sandiwara klasik
clean	bersih
to clean	membersihkan [bersih]
cleaning	pembersihan
clear (understood)	jelas
cliff	jurang
to climb	naik [nail] • mendaki [daki]
cloakroom	tempat penggantungan jas
clock	jam
to close	menutup [tutup]
closed	tutup
clothing (store)	(toko) pakaian
cloud	awan
cloudy	mendung/berawan
clove	cengkeh
clown	pelawak
(night)club	klub (malam)
coast	pantai
coat	jas
cocaine	kokain
coconut	kelapa
coffee	kopi
coins	koin
cold (flu)	pilek/sakit selesma
cold	dingin

It's cold here.
Dingin di sini.
to have a cold
masuk angin

cold water	air dingin
to collapse (thing)	ambruk [ambruk]
colleague	rekan
college	perguruan tinggi
colour	warna
comb	sisir
to come (arrive)	datang [datang] • tiba [tiba]
to come from (origin)	berasal [asal]

Come on!
Mari!, Yuk!

comfortable	nyaman
comics	buku komik
commission	komisi
communion	komuni
companion	kawan/teman
company	
(friends)	teman-teman
(business)	perusahaan
compass	kompas
complain	mengeluh [keluh]
complaint	keluhan
compress	kompres
computer game	permainan komputer
concert	konser
condom	kondom
confession (religious)	pengakuan
to confirm (a booking)	memastikan [pasti]
confirmation	penegasan

Congratulations!
Selamat!

constipation	sukar buang air besar
to be constipated	sukar buang air
construction work	pembuatan
content (happy)	puas
contraceptive	kontrasepsi
convent	biara
to cook	masak [masak]
cool (temperature)	sejuk

Cool!
Keren! (col)

cordial	sirup
corner	sudut
corrupt	korup
cosmetics	dandanan
cost	
(of object)	harga
(of service)	ongkos
cotton	katun
cough (v/n)	batuk
to count	menghitung [hitung]
country	negara
countryside	daerah luar kota
coupon	kupon
court	
(legal)	pengadilan
(tennis)	lapangan tenis

cow sapi
crab kepiting
crafts kerajinan tangan
crafty cerdik
crag (wall of rock) tebing batu yang terjal
crazy gila
credit card kartu kredit
cremation pembakaran mayat • kremasi
cricket (insect) jengkerik
cross
  (angry) marah
  (religious) salib
cross-country trail lari lintas alam
crossroad perempatan
crowded ramai
cucumber ketimun
a cuddle memeluk
cup cangkir
curator kurator
current affairs berita hangat
customs (border) bea dan cukai • pabean
custom (tradition) adat
to cut memotong [potong]
cute (baby) lucu

D

dad ayah/bapak
daily harian
to dance berjoget [joget] • menari [tari] • berdansa [dansa]
dangerous bahaya
dark gelap
date tanggal
date
  (appointment) janji
  (time) tanggal
to date (someone) berpacaran [pacar]
date of birth tanggal kelahiran
daughter anak perempuan
dawn (sunrise) subuh • matahari terbit
day hari

  day after tomorrow
  lusa
  day before yesterday
  kemarin dulu
  in (six) days
  dalam (enam) hari lagi

dead
  (battery/animal) mati
  (person) meninggal
deaf tuli
death kematian
to decide memutuskan [putus]
deep dalam
deer kijang
deforestation penebangan hutan
delay tertunda
delicious enak
delirious gila
democracy demokrasi

D

demonstration	demo
dental floss	benang gigi
dentist	dokter gigi
to deny	menyangkal [sangkal]
deodorant	deodoran
depart	berangkat
department stores	toko serba ada
departure	keberangkatan
to deposit (luggage)	menitipkan [titip]
descendent	keturunan
desert	gurun pasir
design	desain
destination	tempat tujuan
to destroy	merusakkan [rusak]
detail	perincian
develop (film)	mencuci [cuci]
diabetes	kencing manis
diarrhoea	diare/mencret
diary	catatan harian
dice (playing)	dadu
dictionary	kamus
to die (person)	meninggal [tinggal]
die (dice)	dadu
different	berbeda
difficult	sukar/susah
dining car	kereta makan
dinner	makan malam
direct	langsung
director	direktur
(of film)	sutradara
dirty	kotor
disabled	cacat
disadvantage	kerugian
disco	disko
discount	korting/diskon
to discover	menemukan [temu]
discrimination	diskriminasi
disease	penyakit
dismissal	pembubaran
distance (length)	jarak
to dive	menyelam [selam]
diving	selam
diving equipment	alat selam
divorce	cerai
dizzy	pusing
to do	melakukan [laku]

What are you doing?
Sedang buat apa?
I didn't do it.
Bukan saya.

doctor	dokter
documentary	filem dokumenter
dog	anjing
dole	uang sokongan
doll (toy)	boneka
door	pintu
dope (drugs)	ganja
double bed	tempat tidur besar
double room	kamar besar
dozen	lusin
drama (arts)	seni drama
dramatic	dramatis
to dream	mimpi [mimpi]

dress	rok
to dress	memakai [pakai]
drink	minuman
to drink	minum [minum]
to drive	menjalankan [jalan]
drivers licence	SIM (Surat Izin Mengemudi)
drop	jatuh
drug	
(prescription)	obat
(illegal)	obat terlarang
drug addiction	pecandu
drug dealer	pedagang narkotika
drug store	toko obat
drums	gendang/drum
to be drunk	mabuk
dry	kering
to dry	menjemur [jemur]
duck	bebek
dummy (baby's)	dot
during	selama
dust	debu
duty	tugas
dysentery	disentri

E

each	tiap-tiap
ear	telinga
early	pagi-pagi • lekas

It's early.
Masih pagi-pagi.

to earn	mendapat [dapat]
earrings	anting-anting
earth	bumi/dunia
earth (soil)	tanah
earthquake	gempa bumi
east	timur
Easter	Paskah
easy	mudah
eat	makan
economy	ekonomi
economy class	kelas ekonomi
editor	redaktur
to educate	mendidik [didik]
education	pendidikan
egg	telur
elections	pemilihan umum • pemilu
electricity	listrik
elevator	lift
embarassed	malu
embarassment	memalukan
embassy	kedutaan besar
emergency	darurat
employee	pekerja/ karyawan
employer	majikan
empty (adj)	kosong
end	akhir
to end	mengakhiri [akhir]
endangered species	binatang langka
endorsement	pengesahan
engagement	
(appointment)	janji
(wedding)	pertunangan
engine	mesin
engineer	insinyur

engineering	keahlian teknik
English	Inggris
to enjoy (oneself)	menikmati [nikmat]
enough	cukup

Enough!
Sudah cukup!

to enter	masuk [masuk]
entertaining	menghibur [hibur]
entrance	jalan/ pintu masuk
envelope	amplop
environment	lingkungan
epilepsy	epilepsi
equal opportunity	hak yang sama
equality	persamaan
equipment	peralatan
essential	perlu
European	dari Eropa
evening	malam
every	masing-masing
everybody	semua orang
every day	setiap hari
everything	segala sesuatu
example	contoh

For example ...
Misalnya ... • Contohnya ...

excellent	ulung
exchange	penukaran
to exchange	menukarkan [tukar]
exchange rate	kurs
excluded	tidak dimasukkan
excuse	alasan

Excuse me.
Permisi.

to exhibit	memperlihatkan [lihat]
exhibition	pameran
exit	keluar
expensive	mahal
experience	pengalaman
exploitation	eksploitasi
to export	mengekspor [ekspor]
express	ekspres
express mail	pos ekspres/kilat
eye	mata

F

face	muka
factory	pabrik
factory worker	pekerja pabrik
to faint	pingsan [pingsan]
to fall	jatuh
fall (autumn)	musim gugur
family	keluarga
famous	terkenal
fan	
(hand-held)	kipas tangan
(machine)	kipas
(of a team)	penggemar

Fantastic!
Asik!

far	jauh

Is it far?
Jauh?

farm	pertanian/ perkebunan
farmer	petani
fart	kentut
fast	
(quick)	cepat
(n/v)	puasa [puasa]
fat (adj)	gemuk
father	bapak/ayah
father-in-law	bapak mertua
fault (some-one's)	salah
faulty	cacat
fear	ketakutan
to feel	merasa [rasa]
feelings	perasaan
female	
(human)	perempuan
(animal)	betina
fence	pagar
festival	perayaan/pesta
fever	demam
few	beberapa
fiancé(e)	tunangan
fiction	fiksi
field	ladang
fight	pertengkaran
to fight	bertengkar [tengkar]
figures	angka
to fill	mengisi [isi]
film (speed)	(kecepatan) filem
filtered	saring
to find	menemukan [temu]
a fine	denda
finger	jari
finished	habis
fir	cemara
fire	api
firewood	kayu bakar
first	pertama
first class	kelas satu • eksekutif
first-aid kit	kotak pertolong-an pertama
first name	pranama
fish	ikan
to fish	memancing [pancing]
flag	bendera
flashlight (torch)	senter
flat (land, etc)	datar
flea	kutu
flight	penerbangan
floor	
(of room)	lantai
(storey)	tingkat
flour	tepung
flower (seller)	(penjual) bunga
fluent	lancar
fly	lalat
foggy	berkabut
to follow (join in)	mengikuti [ikut]
food	makanan
food stall	warung
foot	kaki
football (soccer)	sepak bola
footpath	jalan kecil • pinggir jalan
for	
(purpose)	untuk/buat
(length of time)	selama

foreign	asing
foreigner	orang asing
forest	hutan
forever	selama-lamanya
to forget	lupa [lupa]

I forget.
Saya lupa.
Forget about it!
Tidak apa-apa!

to forgive	mema'afkan [ma'af]
fork	garpu
fortnight	dua minggu
fortune teller	ahli nujum
foyer	tempat menunggu
free	
(not bound)	bebas
(of charge)	gratis
to freeze	membeku [beku]
fresh	segar
Friday	Hari Jumat
fried	goreng
friend	teman
frog	kodok
from	dari
front	depan
frozen foods	makanan beku
fruit	buah-buahan
full	penuh
full (of food)	kenyang
fun	senang

for fun
untuk bersenang-senang
to have fun
bersenang-senang [senang]
to make fun of
memperolok-olokkan [olok]

funeral	pemakaman
funny	lucu
future	masa depan

G

game	
(boardgame)	mainan
(sport)	pertandingan
game show	kuis
garage	garasi/ bengkel
garbage	sampah
garden	kebun
gardening	berkebun
gardens (botanical)	kebun raya
garlic	bawang putih
gas cartridge	pelor gas
gate	pintu
gay	gay/ homo(seks)
general	umum
generous	murah hati
gentle	lembut
geography	ilmu bumi

Get lost!
Pergi!

giant	raksasa
gift	hadiah/kado
girl	perempuan
girlfriend	pacar (perempuan)
give	memberi [beri]

Could you give me ...?
Tolong kasih ...

glad senang
glass gelas
glasses (eye) kaca mata
glue lem
to go pergi [pergi]

Let's go.
Ayo kita pergi.
We'd like to go to ...
Kami ingin pergi ke ...
Go straight ahead.
Terus.
to go out with
bersama dengan
to go home
pulang

goal gol
goalkeeper kiper
goat kambing
God Tuhan • Allah (Muslim)
gold emas

of gold
dibuat dari emas

good baik
goods (possessions) barang

Good afternoon.
Selamat sore.

Goodbye.
(leaving) Selamat tinggal.
(staying) Selamat jalan.
(inf) Daag/Mari.

Good evening.
Selamat malam.
Good luck!
Selamat!
Good morning.
Selamat pagi.
Good night.
Selamat malam.

government pemerintah
gram gram
grammar tatabahasa
grandchild cucu
grandfather kakek
grandmother nenek
grape anggur
graphic art seni grafik
grass rumput
grave kuburan

Great!
Bagus!

green hijau
greengrocer penjual sayuran dan buah-buahan
grey abu-abu
ground tanah
group kelompok
to guess menerka [terka]
guest tamu
guide (person or audio) pemandu
guidebook buku pedoman
guidedog anjing penuntun
guided trek jalan yang dipandu
guinea pig marmot

guitar — gitar
gymnastics — olahraga senam

H

habit — kebiasaan
hair — rambut
hairbrush — sikat rambut
half — setengah

half a litre
setengah liter

to hallucinate — menghayalkan [khayal]
ham — daging babi
hammer — palu
hammock — buaian
hand — tangan
handbag — tas tangan
handicrafts — kerajinan tangan
handmade — buatan tangan
handsome (male) — tampan/ganteng
happy — gembira/senang

Happy birthday!
Selamat hari ulang tahun!

harbour — pelabuhan
hard
  (not soft) — keras
  (difficult) — sukar/susah
harassment — gangguan
hashish — ganja
hat — topi
to have — ada [ada] • punya [punya] • dapat [dapat]

Do you have ...?
Apakah ... ada?
I have ...
Saya punya ...

he — dia
head — kepala
headache — sakit kepala
health — kesehatan
healthy — sehat
to hear — mendengar [dengar]
hearing aid — alat bantu-dengar
heart — jantung
heat — kepanasan
heater — alat pemanas
heavy — berat

Hello.
Halo/Salam.

helmet — helm
to help — membantu [bantu]

Help!
Tolong!

herbs — jamu
herbalist — ahli jamu
here — di sini
heroin (addict) — (pecandu) heroin
high — tinggi
high blood pressure — tekanan darah tinggi
high school — sekolah menengah atas (SMA)

to hike — berjalan kaki [jalan]
hiking — jalan di hutan
hiking boots — sepatu jalan
hiking route — rute jalan
hill — bukit
Hindu — Hindu
to hire (rent) — menyewa [sewa]
historical ruins — runtuhan bersejarah
history — sejarah
to hitchhike — menggonceng [gonceng]
HIV positive — HIV positif
hobby — hobi/kegemaran
hole — lobang
holiday — liburan
Holy Week — minggu suci
homeless — tunawisma • orang jalanan
homosexual — gay • homo(seks)
honest — terus terang
honey — madu
honeymoon — bulan madu
horn (animal) — tanduk
horny — gatal
horrible — mengerikan
horse (riding) — kuda (tunggang)
hospital — rumah sakit
hospitality — keramah-tamahan
hot
(temperature) — panas
(spicy) — pedas

It's hot here.
Panas di sini.

to be hot — kepanasan [panas]
hot water — air panas
hotel — hotel
hour — jam
house — rumah
housework — pekerjaan rumah tangga
how — bagaimana

How can I get to ...?
Naik apa saya bisa ke ...?
How do you say ... in Indonesian?
Apa bahasa Indonesianya ...?
How many? (animals)
Berapa ekor?
How many? (goods)
Berapa buah?
How much?
Berapa?

hug — peluk
human rights — hak asasi manusia (HAM)
humid — lembab
a hundred — seratus
hungry — lapar
to hunt — berburu [buru]
husband — suami

I

I — saya/aku

I'm Chris.
Saya Chris.

ice — es
ice cream — es krim
idea — ide

identification	surat keterangan
identification card	KTP (Kartu Tanda Penduduk)
idiot	bodoh
if	kalau
ill	sakit
imagine	membayangkan
immediately	dengan segara
immigration	imigrasi
important	penting

It's (not) important.
(Tidak) penting.

in	dalam

in a hurry
terburu-buru

in front of	di depan
included	termasuk
income tax	pajak penghasilan
incomprehensible	tidak dapat dimengerti
indicator	penunjuk
indigenous	asli
indigestion	salah cerna
Indonesia	Indonesia
Indonesian	Bahasa Indonesia

I (don't) speak Indonesian.
Saya (tidak) berbahasa Indonesia.

industry	industri
inequality	ketidaksamaan
infection	infeksi
information	keterangan
to inject	menyuntikkan [suntik]
injection	jarum suntik
injury	luka
insect	serangga
inside	di dalam
instructor	pelatih
insurance	asuransi
intense	hebat
interesting	menarik
intermission	istirahat
international	internasional
intersection	persimpangan
interview	wawancara
island	pulau
itch	gatal
itinerary	rencana perjalanan
ivory	gading

J

jacket	jaket
jackfruit	nangka
jail	penjara
jar	toples
jealous	iri hati
jeans	jean
jeep	jip
jewellery	perhiasan
Jewish	Yahudi
job	pekerjaan
job advertisement	iklan pekerjaan
job description	deskripsi pekerjaan
jockey	joki
joke	lelucon
to joke	bercanda [canda]

journalist — wartawan
journey — perjalanan
judge (court) — hakim
juice — jus • air buah
jump
  (across) — lompat
  (high) — loncat
jumper (sweater) — sweater
just (completed) — baru

  just one
  satu saja

justice — keadilan

K

key — kunci
keyboard — papan mata
kick — tendangan [tendang]
kick off — memulai [mulai]
to kill — membunuh [bunuh]
kilogram — kilogram
kilometre — kilometer
kind (adj) — baik-hati
kindergarten — taman kanak-kanak
king — raja
kiosk — kios
kiss — cium
to kiss — mencium [cium]
kitchen — dapur
kitten — anak kucing
knapsack — ransel
knee — lutut
knife — pisau
to know
  (someone) — kenal [kenal]
  (something) — tahu [tahu]

  I don't know.
  Saya tidak tahu.

L

lace — renda
lake — danau
lamb — anak domba
land (ground) — tanah
landscape — lanskap
language — bahasa
large — luas
last (final) — terakhir

  last month
  bulan yang lalu
  last night
  tadi malam
  last week
  minggu yang lalu
  last year
  tahun yang lalu

late (not on time) — terlambat
later — nanti
laugh — tertawa [tawa]
laundry — binatu
law — hukum
lawyer — ahli hukum • advokat
laxatives — obat pencahar
lay down — berbaring
lazy — malas
leader — pemimpin

leak — bocor
to learn — belajar [ajar]
leather — kulit
leathergoods — kerajinan kulit
lecture — kuliah
lecturer — dosen
ledge (cliff) — jurang

to be left (behind/over)
ditinggalkan [tinggal]

left (not right) — kiri
left-handed — kidal
left luggage — barang yang ditinggalkan
left-wing — orang sayap kiri
leg
(body) — kaki
(in race) — taraf
legalisation — legalisasi
legislation — perundang-undangan
lemon — jeruk nipis
length — panjang
lens — lensa
Lent — bulan puasa Masehi
lesbian — lesbi/homo
less — kurang
letter — surat
liar — pembohong
library — perpustakaan
lice — kutu
to lie — membohong [bohong]
life — hidup
lift (elevator) — lift
light
(electric) — lampu
(not dark) — terang
(not heavy) — ringan
light bulb — bola lampu
light meter — meteran lampu
lighter — geretan
to like — suka [suka]
line — garis
lips — bibir
lipstick — gincu
to listen — mendengar [dengar]
little
(small) — kecil
(amount) — sedikit
to live
(life) — hidup [hidup]
(somewhere) — tinggal [tinggal]
liver — hati
local — lokal
local (city) bus — bis kota
location — tempat
lock — kunci
to lock — mengunci [kunci]
long
(measurement) — panjang
(time) — lama
long distance — interlokal
long-distance bus — bis antar kota

Long live ...!
Dirgahayu ...!

to look — melihat [lihat]

to look after
memelihara [pelihara]
to look for
mencari [cari]

loose	longgar
loose change	recehan
to lose (something)	menghilangkan [hilang]
loser	orang yang kalah
loss	kalah/rugi
lost	tersesat
a lot (quantity)	banyak
lotion	cairan
loud	keras
lounge (room)	ruang tamu
love	kasih/cinta/ sayang

I love you.
Saya cinta kamu.

lover	kekasih
low	rendah
low blood pressure	tekanan darah rendah
loyal	setia
luck	untung
lucky	beruntung
luggage	bagasi
luggage lockers	lemari
lunch	makan siang
lunchtime	waktu makan siang
luxury	mewah

M

machine	mesin
mad	
(angry)	marah
(crazy)	gila
made (of)	dibuat (dari)
magazine	majalah
magician	tukang sihir
mail	pos
mailbox	kotak pos
main	utama
main road	jalan raya
main square	lapangan • alun-alun
majority	mayoritas
to make	membuat [buat]
make-up	dandanan
malaria	malaria
male	
(person)	laki-laki
(animal)	jantan
man	orang laki-laki • pria
manager	pemimpin
mango	mangga
manual worker	pekerja/buruh
many	banyak
map	peta

Can you show me on the map?
Tolong tunjukkan di peta.

marijuana	ganja
marital status	status kawin
market	pasar
marriage	perkawinan/ pernikahan
marry	menikah/kawin
marvellous	bagus sekali
mask (face)	topeng
mass (church)	misa
massage	pijit
to massage	memijit [pijit]
mat	tikar

match (sport) pertandingan
matches korek api
material (for clothing) bahan baju

It doesn't matter.
Tidak apa-apa.
What's the matter?
Ada apa?

mattress kasur
may (can) boleh/minta
maybe mungkin
mayor walikota
meaning arti/makna

What does it mean?
Apa artinya?

meat daging
mechanic montir
medal medali
medicine obat
meditation meditasi
to meet bertemu/ketemu [temu]
meeting pertemuan/rapat
member anggota
menstruation menstruasi
menthol (cigarettes) (rokok) mentol
menu daftar makanan
message pesan
metal logam
meteor meteor
metre meter
midnight tengah malam
migraine sakit kepala berat
military service berdinas militer
milk susu
millimetre milimeter
million juta
mineral water (with/without gas) air (soda/putih)
minibus bemo/angkot
minute menit

Just a minute.
Sebentar.
in (five) minutes
dalam (lima) menit lagi

mirror cermin/kaca
miscarriage keguguran
to miss (feel absence) rindu [rindu]
Miss (used for a female younger than you) Mbak
mistake salah
misunderstanding salah paham
to mix campur [campur]
mobile phone ponsel • telpon genggam
modem modem
moisturising cream krim pelembab
monastery biara
Monday Hari Senin
money uang
monk biarawan
monkey kera/monyet
month bulan

this month
bulan ini

monument	monumen
moon	bulan
more	lebih
morning	pagi
Moslem	orang Islam
mosque	mesjid
mosquito	nyamuk
mosquito net	kelambu
most (the)	(yang) paling
mother	ibu
mother-in-law	ibu mertua
motorboat	perahu motor
motorcycle	sepeda motor
motorway (tollway)	jalan tol
mountain	gunung
mountain bike	sepeda gunung
mountaineering	mendaki gunung
mountain hut	pondok
mountain path	jalan gunung
mountain range	pegunungan
mouse	tikus
mouth	mulut
movie	filem
Mr	Bapak/Tuan
Mrs	Ibu
much	banyak
mud	lumpur
mum	Ibu
muscle	otot
museum	musium
music	musik
musician	pemain musik
Muslim	Muslim
must	harus
mute	bisu
mutton	daging domba

N

name	nama

What's your name?
Siapa nama Anda?

napkin	serbet
nappy	popok
nappy rash	ruam
nationality	kebangsaan
national park	taman nasional
nature	alam
nausea	mual
near	dekat

Is it near here?
Dekat dari sini?

necessary	perlu
necklace	kalung
need	perlu/butuh
needle (sewing/ syringe)	jarum
neighbour	tetangga
neither	tidak ada
nervous	gelisah
net	jala
never	tidak pernah
never mind	tidak apa-apa
new	baru
news	berita
newspaper	koran
New Year's Day	Hari Tahun Baru
New Year's Eve	Malam Tahun Baru

next	yang berikutnya
next month	
bulan yang mendatang	
Next time.	
Lain kali.	
next to	
di samping	
next week	
minggu yang mendatang	
next year	
tahun yang mendatang	
nice	baik
nickname	nama panggilan
night	malam
Saturday night	
malam minggu	
night market	pasar malam
no	tidak
noise	bunyi
noisy	ribut
non-direct	tidak langsung
none	tidak satu pun
nonsense	tidak masuk akal
noodles	mie
noon	tengah hari
north	utara
nose	hidung
not	bukan
notebook	buku catatan
nothing	tidak ada apa-apa
not yet	belum
novel (book)	novel/roman
now	sekarang
nuclear energy	tenaga nuklir
nuclear testing	percobaan nuklir
nude	telanjang
number	nomor
nun	biarawati
nurse	jururawat
nut (food)	kacang

O

object	benda
obvious	jelas
occupation	pekerjaan
ocean	laut
odd	
(number)	ganjil
(strange)	aneh
offense	
(personal)	menyinggung perasaan
(legal)	pelanggaran
offer	tawaran
office (work)	(tugas) kantor
office worker	pekerja kantor/ pergawai
offside	offside
often	sering
oil	
(cooking)	minyak
(crude)	oli
OK.	
OK/Baik.	
old	
(person)	tua
(building)	lama

older ... kakak ...
  brother laki-laki
  sister perempuan

Olympic Games Pertandingan Olympiade
on (location) di

  on time
  tepat

once satu kali • sekali
once again sekali lagi
one satu
one-way (ticket) (tiket) satu jalan
onion bawang bombay
only hanya
open buka
to open membuka [buka]
opening (of a play) pembukaan
operation operasi
(telephone) operator penghubung (telpon)
opinion pendapat
opposite lawan
or atau
oral lisan
orange
  (colour) oranye/jingga
  (food) jeruk
orchestra orkes
to order memesan [pesan]
ordinary biasa
to organise mengatur [atur]
orgasm syahwat
original asli
other lain
outgoing (adj) ramah tamah
outside luar
over di seberang
overcoat mantel
overdose terlalu banyak takaran
over here di sini
over there di sana
owe berhutang
owner pemilik
oxygen oksigen
ozone layer lapisan ozon

P

pacifier (dummy) dot
package paket
packet bungkus
padlock kunci kura-kura
page (in book) halaman
pain sakit

  pain in the neck
  menyusahkan

painful menyakitkan
painkillers penawar sakit
to paint
  (a picture) melukis [lukis]
  (a wall) mencat [cat]
painter (artist) pelukis
painting
  (the art) melukis
  (picture) lukisan
pair (a couple) sepasang
palace istana
pap smear papsmir
paper kertas

P

paraplegic	cacat kaki
parcel	paket/ bungkusan
parents	orang tua
park (national)	taman (nasional)
parliament	parlamen/DPR
part (n)	bagian
to part	membagi [bagi]
party	
(fiesta)	pesta
(political)	partai
pass (n)	pas
to pass (give)	memberi [beri]
passenger	penumpang
passive	pasif
passport (number)	(nomor) paspor
past (before)	dulu • yang lalu
path	jalan kecil
patient (adj)	sabar
pawpaw	papaya
to pay	membayar [bayar]
payment	bayaran
peace	damai
peak (of mountain)	puncak
peanut	kacang
pedestrian	pejalan kaki
pen	pena
penalty	hukuman
pencil	pensil
penis	zakar
penknife	pisau lipat
pensioner	pensiunan
people	orang-orang • rakyat
pepper	lada/merica
percent	persen
perfect	sempurna
performance	pertunjukan
performance art	seni pertunjukan
perhaps	barangkali/ mungkin
period pain	sakit menstruasi
permanent	tetap
permanent collection	kumpulan tetap
permission	izin
permit	izin
person	orang
personality	kepribadian
to perspire	berkeringat [keringat]
petition	petisi
petrol	bensin
pharmacy	apotik
phone book	buku telpon
phone box	boks telpon
phonecard	kartu telpon
photo	foto

May I take a photo?
Boleh saya potret?

photograph	foto
photographer	tukang potret
photography	fotografi
pick(axe)	beliung
to pick up	memungut [pungut]
pickpocket	copet
picture	gambar
piece	potong

pig	babi
pill	pil
the Pill	pil kontrasepsi
pillow	bantal
pillowcase	sarung bantal
pinball	main jackpot
pine (tree)	cemara
pineapple	nanas/nenas
pink	merah muda
pipe (plumbing)	pipa
piss	kencing
to piss	buang air kecil
place	tempat
place of birth	tempat kelahiran
plain (adj)	sederhana
plan	rencana
(aero)plane	pesawat terbang/udara
planet	planet
plant	tanaman
to plant	menanam [tanam]
plastic	plastik
plate	piring
plateau	dataran tinggi
platform	peron
play (theatre)	sandiwara
to play	
(a game)	bermain [main]
(music)	main

to play cards
main kartu

player	pemain
playing cards	kartu (main)
please	silakan/tolong
plug (electricity)	steker
plus	tambah
pocket	kantung
poetry	puisi
to point	menunjuk [tunjuk]
poisonous	beracun
poker (the game)	poker
police	polisi
political speech	pidato politik
politicians	politikus
politics	politik
poll (opinion)	jajak (pendapat)
pollen	serbuk sari
pollution	polusi
pool	
(swimming)	kolam renang
(game)	bilyar
poor	miskin
popular	terkenal
pork	daging babi
port (harbour)	pelabuhan
portrait sketcher	pelukis potret
possible	boleh

It's not possible.
Tidak boleh, dilarang.

possibly	mungkin
postage	perangko
postcard	kartu pos
postcode	kode pos
poster	plakat
post office	kantor pos
pot	
(cooking)	panci
(dope)	ganja
potato	kentang
pottery	tembikar
poverty	kemiskinan

power	kuasa
prayer	doa/sembayang
prayer book	buku doa
prefer	lebih suka
pregnant	hamil
prehistoric art	seni prasejarah
premenstrual tension	ketegangan sebelum menstruasi
to prepare	menyiapkan [siap]
prescription	resep
present	
(gift)	kado/hadiah
(time)	sekarang
presentation	penampilan
presenter (TV, etc)	penyiar
president	presiden
pressure	tekanan
pretty (adj)	cantik
prevent	mencegah
price	
(of goods)	harga
(of a service)	ongkos
pride	bangga
priest	
(Catholic)	pastor/romo
(Protestant)	pendeta
prime minister	perdana menteri
a print (artwork)	cetakan
prison	penjara
prisoner	orang hukuman
private	pribadi
private hospital	rumah sakit swasta
privatisation	privatisasi
problem	masalah
to produce	memproduksi [produksi]
producer	penghasil
profession	pekerjaan
profit	untung
profitability	keuntungan
program (TV)	acara
projector	proyektor
promise	janji
proposal	usulan
prostitute	kupu-kupu malam • sundal
to protect	melindungi [lindung]
protected forest	hutan lindung
protected species	spesies dilindungi
to protest	memprotes [protes]
Protestant	Protestan
public toilet	WC umum
to pull	menarik [tarik]
pump	pompa
puncture	kebocoran/pecah
to punish	menyiksa [siksa]
... puppet	wayang ...
leather	kulit
wooden	golek
puppy	anak anjing
pure	murni
purple	ungu
purse	dompet
push	mendorong [dorong]
to put	menyimpan [simpan]

Q

qualifications	kwalifikasi
quality	kwalitas/mutu
quantity	jumlah
quarantine	karantina
quarrel	pertengkaran
quarter	perempat
queen	ratu
question	pertanyaan
to question	bertanya [tanya]
queue	antri
quick	cepat
quickly	dengan cepat
quiet	sepi, tenang
quinine	kina
to quit	berhenti [henti]

R

rabbit	kelinci
race	
(breed)	ras
(sport)	perlombaan
racing bike	balap sepeda
racism	rasisme
racquet	raket
radiator	radiator
railroad	jalan kereta
railway station	stasiun kereta
rain	hujan

It's raining heavily.
Hujan deras.

rally (demonstration)	demo
rape	perkosaan
rare (uncommon)	jarang
a rash	ruam
rat	tikus besar
rate of pay	tarif • kurs • bea
raw (food)	mentah
razor	alat cukur
razor blade	silet
to read	membaca [baca]
ready	siap
to realise	menyadari [sadar]
reason	alasan
receipt	kwitansi
receive	menerima
recent	baru saja
to recognise	mengakui [akui]
to recommend	menasehati [nasehat]
recording	rekam
recycle	mendaur ulang
red	merah
referee	wasit
reference	referensi
reflection	
(mirror)	bayangan
(thought)	pemikiran
reforestation	reboisasi
refrigerator	lemari es • kultas
refugee	pengungsi
refund	pembayaran kembali
to refuse	menolak [tolak]
region	wilayah
regional	daerah
registered mail	pos tercatat
to regret	menyesal [sesal]
relationship	hubungan

to relax	bersantai [santai]
religion	agama
religious	beragama
remember	ingat [ingat]
remote	pelosok
to rent	menyewa [sewa]
to repair	memperbaiki [baik]
repeat	mengulangi [ulang]
reply	balasan
to reply	membalas [balas]
to report	melaporkan [lapor]
republic	republik
to request	minta [minta] • mohon [mohon]
reservation	pesanan tempat
to reserve	memesan [pesan]
resignation	pengunduran diri
respect	hormat
responsibility	tanggung jawab
rest	
(relaxation)	istirahat
(what's left)	sisa
to rest	beristirahat [istirahat]
restaurant	rumah makan • restoran
result	hasil
resumé	riwayat hidup
retired	pensiun
return	kembali
return (ticket)	(tiket) pulang-pergi
review	tinjauan
rheumatism	encok
rhythm	irama
rice	
(cooked)	nasi
(uncooked)	beras
rich	
(food)	gurih
(wealthy)	kaya
to ride (horse, bus, etc)	naik
right	
(correct)	benar
(not left)	kanan

You're right.
Anda benar.

right now	segera
right-wing	sayap kanan
ring	
(on finger)	cincin
(sound)	bunyi

I'll give you a ring.
Nanti saya telpon.

ripe	matang
a rip-off	terlalumahal
risk	risiko
river	sungai/kali
road	jalan
road map	peta jalan
roasted	panggang
to rob	merampok [rampok]
rock	batu
(wall of) rock	tebing
rock climbing	panjat tebing

rock group	band musik
rolling	gelinding
romance	percintaan
roof	atap
room (number)	(nomor) kamar
rope	tali/tambang
rotten	busuk/rusak
round (shape)	bulat
(at the) roundabout	(di) bundaran
rowing	mendayung
rubbish	sampah
rug	permadani
ruins	runtuhan
rules	peraturan
run	lari [lari]

S

sad	sedih
safe	
(secure)	aman
(vault)	peti besi
safe sex	seks aman
sail	layar
sailor	pelaut
saint	orang suci
salary	gaji
(on) sale	obral
sales department	bagian penjualan
salt	garam
salty	asin
same	sama
sand	pasir
sandals	sandal
sanitary napkins	pembalut wanita
Saturday	Hari Sabtu
to save	menyelamatkan [selamat]
to say	berkata [kata] • bilang [bilang]
to scale (climb)	naik [naik] • mendaki [daki]
scared	takut
scarf	syal • selendang • jilbab
scenery	pemandangan
school	sekolah
science	ilmu/sains
scientist	ilmuwan
scissors	gunting
to score	membuat angka [buat]
scoreboard	papan angka
screen (film)	layar
script	naskah
sculpture	seni ukir
sea	laut
to search	mencari [cari]
seasick	mabuk laut
seaside	tepi laut
season	musim
seat	tempat duduk • kursi
seat belt	sabuk pengaman
second	
(unit of time)	detik
(in order)	kedua
second class	kelas dua/ bisnis
secretary	sekretaris
see	lihat

I see. (understand)
Saya mengerti. • Paham.
See you later.
Sampai jumpa.
See you tomorrow.
Sampai jumpa besok.

seldom	jarang
self-employed	pekerja bebas
selfish	egois
self-service	pelayanan sendiri
to sell	menjual [jual]
to send	mengirim [kirim]
sense	akal
sensible	bijaksana
sentence	
(words)	kalimat
(prison)	hukuman
to separate	memisahkan [pisah]
series	seri
serious	serius
servant	pembantu
to serve	melayani [layan]
service	
(assistance)	jasa
(charge)	ongkos
(religious)	misa
several	beberapa
sew	jahit
sex	seks
sexism	seksisme
sexy	seksi
shade	teduh
shampoo	sampo
to shampoo	mengeramas [keramas]
shape	bentuk
to share (with)	bersama-sama

to share a dorm
bersama-sama di kamar

shave	cukur
she	dia
sheep	domba
sheet	
(bed)	seprei
(of paper)	halaman
shell (sea)	kerang
shelves	rak
ship	kapal
shirt	kemeja
shit	kotoran/tinja
to shit	buang air besar [buang]
shoelaces	tali sepatu
shoes	sepatu
shoe shop	toko sepatu
to shoot	menembak [tembak]
shop	toko
to go shopping	berbelanja [belanja]
short (length/ height)	pendek
short film	filem pendek
short story	cerita pendek
shortage	kekurangan
shorts (clothes)	celana pendek
shoulders	bahu
to shout	berteriak [teriak]

show pertunjukan
to show menunjukan [tunjuk]

Please show me (on the map).
Tolong tunjukkan (di peta).

shower mandi • air dus
shrimp udang
shrine tempat suci
shut tutup
shy malu
sick sakit
sickness penyakit
side (of a street) pinggir
sign tanda
to sign menandatangani [tanda]
signature tanda tangan
silk sutra
silver perak

of silver
dari perak

similar mirip
simple sederhana
sin dosa
since sejak
to sing menyanyi [nyanyi]
singer penyanyi
singer-songwriter pencipta lagu
single (unique) unik
single room kamar untuk seorang
... sister ... perempuan
older kakak
younger adik

to sit duduk [duduk]
size ukuran•besaran
to ski main ski
skiing main ski
skin kulit
skinny kurus
sky langit
sleazy (person) genit
to sleep tidur [tidur]
sleeping bag tas tidur
sleeping car kereta tidur
sleeping pills obat tidur
sleepy ngantuk
to slice mengiris [iris]
slide (film) slide
slow pelan
small kecil
smell bau
to smell mencium [cium]
to smile tersenyum [senyum]
smoke asap
to smoke merokok [rokok]
snake ular
soap sabun
soap opera sinetron
soccer sepak bola
social-democratic sosial-demokratis
social sciences ilmu sosial
social security (payment) jaminan sosial
social welfare kesejahteraan sosial
socialist sosialis
society masyarakat
socks kaos kaki

soft	lembut
solid	padat
some	beberapa
somebody	seseorang
something	sesuatu
sometimes	kadang-kadang
son	anak laki-laki
song	lagu
soon	segera
sorry	ma'af

I'm sorry.
Ma'af.

sound	suara, bunyi
sour	asam
south	selatan
souvenir	oleh-oleh • kenang-kenan-gan • cendera mata
souvenir shop	toko oleh-oleh
soy sauce	kecap asin
space (area)	tempat
speak	bicara
to speak (Indonesian)	berbahasa Indonesia [bahasa]
special	istimewa/spesial
specialist	ahli
speed (limit)	(batas) kecepatan
spicy	pedas
spoon	sendok
sport	olahraga
sportsman	olahragawan
sportsplayer	pemain olahraga
sportswoman	olahragawati
a sprain	keseleo
spring	
(season)	musim bunga/ semi
(coil)	per
square	
(shape)	persegi
(plaza)	alun-alun• lapangan
stadium	stadion
stage	panggung
stairs	tangga
stairway	tangga
stale	busuk
stamp	perangko
standard (usual)	standar•biasa
standard of living	tingkat kehidupan
starfruit	belimbing
stars (in the sky)	bintang
to start	mulai [mulai]
station	stasiun/terminal
stationmaster	kepala stasiun
statue	patung
to stay	
(remain)	tinggal [tinggal]
(overnight)	inap [menginap]
to steal	mencuri [curi]
steam	uap
steep	
(hill)	curam
(price)	tinggi
step	langkah
still (yet)	masih
stomach	perut
stomachache	sakit perut

DICTIONARY

stone	batu
stoned (drugged)	mabuk
to stop	berhenti [henti]

Stop!
Stop! • Berhenti! • Kiri!

storm	badai
story	cerita
stove	kompor
straight (line)	lurus
strange	aneh
stranger	orang tidak dikenal
stream (small river)	kali
street	jalan
strength	kekuatan
(on) strike	mogok
string	tali
stroll	jalan-jalan
strong	kuat
stubborn	keras kepala
student	
(school)	pelajar
(university)	mahasiswa
studio	studio
stupid	bodoh
style	gaya
subtitles	teks
suburb	pinggir kota

suburbs of Jakarta
pinggir kota Jakarta

success	sukses
to suffer	menderita [derita]
sugar	gula
suitcase	kopor
summer	musim panas
sun	matahari
sunblock	krim terbakar matahari
sunburnt	kulit terbakar
Sunday	Hari Minggu
sunglasses	kaca mata hitam
sunny	cerah
sunrise	matahari terbit
sunset	matahari terbenam
supermarket	pasar swalayan

Sure.
Betul.

surface mail	pos biasa
to surf	berselancar [selancar]
surfboard	papan selancar
surname	nama keluarga
a surprise	keheranan
to survive	selamat [selamat] • hidup [hidup]
to sweat	berkeringat [keringat]
sweet (adj)	manis
sweets	permen
to swim	berenang [renang]
swimming pool	kolam renang
swimsuit	baju renang
sword	pedang
sympathetic	simpatik
synagogue	gereja Yahudi
synthetic	buatan
syringe	jarum suntik

T

table	meja
tablet	tablet
table tennis	tenis meja
tail (of animal)	ekor
tailor	penjahit
to take	
(away)	mengambil [ambil]
(the train)	naik [naik]

to take off (depart)
berangkat [angkat]
to take photographs
ambil photo

to talk (chat)	bercakap [cakap]
tall	tinggi
tampon	tampon
taste	rasa
tasty	enak
tax	pajak
taxi (stand)	(pangkalan) taksi
tea	teh
teacher	guru
teaching	mengajar
team (sport)	regu
tear (crying)	air mata
technique	teknik
teeth	gigi
telegram	kawat/telegram
telephone	telpon
to telephone	menelpon [telpon]
telephone office	kantor/kios telpon • wartel
telescope	teleskop
television	televisi
to tell (inform)	memberitahu [tahu]
teller	kasir
temperature	
(fever)	demam
(weather)	suhu udara
temple	
(Buddhist)	candi
(Chinese)	kelenteng
(Hindu)	pura
tennis (court)	(lapangan) tenis
tent (pegs)	(pasak untuk) tenda
tenth	kesepuluh
terrible	buruk sekali
test (exam)	ujian
to thank	mengucapkan terima kasih [ucap]

Thank you.
Terima kasih.

that	itu
theatre (play)	gedung sandiwara
there	
(distant)	di sana
(nearby)	di situ

there is/are
ada

they	mereka
thick	tebal
thief	perampok/ maling
thin	tipis
to think	berpikir [pikir]

third	ketiga
thirsty	haus
this	ini
thought	pikiran
thread	benang
throat	tenggorokan
Thursday	Hari Kamis
ticket	karcis
ticket collector	kenek • pemungut karcis
ticket office	loket
tide	pasang
tiger	harimau
tight	sempit
time	jam

What time is it?
Jam berapa?

timetable	daftar waktu • jadwal
tin (can)	kaleng
tin opener	pembuka kaleng
tip (gratuity)	tip
tired	lelah
tissues	tisu
to	ke
toad	kodok
toast (bread)	roti bakar
tobacco	tembakau
today	hari ini
together	sama-sama
toilet paper	kertas kloset • tisu
toilet	kamar kecil
tomorrow	besok

tomorrow afternoon
besok sore

tomorrow morning
besok pagi

tongue	lidah
tonight	malam ini
too	
(excessive)	terlalu
(as well)	juga

too expensive
terlalu mahal
too many/much
terlalu banyak

tool	alat
tooth	gigi
tooth (front)	gigi (depan)
tooth (back)	gigi (belakang)
toothache	sakit gigi
toothbrush	sikat gigi
toothpaste	odol • pasta gigi
torch (flashlight)	senter
to touch	menyentuh [sentuh]
tour	berkeliling
tourist	turis
tourist information office	kantor parawisata/ informasi
toward	ke arah
towel	handuk
tower	menara
toxic waste	sisa buangan toksik
track	
(footprints)	jejak
(sports)	olahraga lari
(path)	jalan kecil
trade union	serikat buruh

traffic	lalu-lintas
traffic jam	macet
traffic lights	lampu lalu-lintas • lampu merah
trail (route)	jalan
train	kereta api
train station	stasiun kereta
tram	trem
transit lounge	tempat transit
to translate	menerjemahkan [terjemah]
to travel	jalan-jalan
travel agency	agen perjalanan
travel book	buku perjalanan
travellers cheque	cek turis
travel sickness	mabuk jalan
tree	pohon
trek	perjalanan
trip (journey)	perjalanan
trousers	celana panjang
truck	truk
true	benar

It's true.
Benar.

to trust	percaya [percaya]
truth	kebenaran
to try (attempt)	mencoba [coba]
T-shirt	T-shirt
Tuesday	Hari Selasa
tune (song)	lagu
turn	belok

Turn left/right.
Belok kiri/kanan.

TV	televisi
twice	dua kali
twin beds	tempat tidur kembar
twins	kembar
type (of product)	macam/jenis
to type	mengetik [ketik]
typhoid	demam tipus
typical	khas
tyre	ban

U

umbrella	payung
under	di bawah
to understand	mengerti [mengerti]

I (don't) understand.
Saya (tidak) mengerti.

underwear	celana dalam
unemployed	penganggur
unemployment	mengangguran
unions	serikat sekerja
universe	semesta alam
university	universitas
unripe	mentah
unsafe	tidak aman
until (June)	sampai (Juni)
unusual	luar biasa
up	naik
uphill (road)	naik
urgent	penting
useful	berguna
usual	biasa

V

vacant	kosong
vacation	liburan
vaccination	pencacaran
valley	lembah
valuable	berharga
value (price)	nilai
van	gerbong
vegetables	sayur-sayuran
vegetarian	
(person)	vegetarian
(food)	nabati

I'm vegetarian.
Saya vegetarian.

vegetation	tumbuh-tumbuhan
vein	urat darah
venereal disease	penyakit kelamin
very	sangat
video tape	kaset video
view	pemandangan
village	desa/ kampung
virus	virus
visa	visa
to visit	mengunjungi [kunjung]
vitamin	vitamin
voice	suara
volcano	gunung api
volume (sound)	suara
vomit (n/v)	muntah
to vote	memberikan suara [beri]
vulgar	kasar

W

wait	tunggu
waiter	pelayan
waiting room	kamar tunggu
to wake up	bangun [bangun]
to walk	jalan kaki [jalan]
wall	
(inside)	dinding
(outside)	tembok
to want	mau [mau] • ingin [ingin]
war	perang
wardrobe	lemari
warm	hangat
to warn	memperingatkan [ingat]
to wash	
(yourself)	mandi [mandi]
(something)	mencuci [cuci]
washing machine	mesin cuci
watch (for wrist)	jam [tangan]
to watch	menonton [tonton]

Watch out!
Hati-hati! • Awas!

... water	air ...
boiled	matang
mineral	mineral
purified	putih
water bottle	botol air
waterfall	air terjun
watermelon	semangka

waves — ombak
way — jalan

Please tell me the way to ...
Tolong, jalan yang mana ke ...?
Which way?
Jalan mana?
Way Out.
Keluar.

we
(incl) — kita
(excl) — kami (see Grammar, page 24)

weak — lemah
wealthy — kaya
to wear — memakai [pakai]
weather — cuaca
wedding — perkawinan/ pernikahan
wedding cake — kue pengantin
wedding present — hadiah pernikahan
Wednesday — Hari Rabu
week — minggu

this week
minggu ini

weekend — akhir minggu
to weigh — menimbang [timbang]
weight — berat

Welcome.
Selamat datang.
You're welcome.
Kembali. Sama-sama.

welfare — kesejahteraan
well (healthy) — sehat
west — barat
westerner (col) — bule
wet — basah
what — apa

What?
Apa?
What's he saying?
Dia bilang apa?
What is that?
Apa itu?
What's your name?
Siapa nama Anda?
What time is it?
Jam berapa sekarang?

wheel — roda
wheelchair — kursi roda
when
(past) — waktu
(future) — waktu nanti

When?
Kapan? Bilamana?
When does (the train) leave?
Kapan (keretanya) berangkat?
Where?
Di mana?
Where's the bank?
Banknya di mana?

which — yang mana
while (currently) — sedang
white — putih
who — siapa

Who?
Siapa?

Who's calling?
Siapa yang menelpon?
Who is it?
Siapa ini?
Who are they?
Mereka siapa?

whole (all) seluruh
why kenapa/mengapa

Why?
Mengapa? Kenapa?
Why is the bank closed?
Kenapa banknya tutup?

wide lebar
wife istri
wild animal binatang buas
to win menang [menang]
wind angin
window jendela

to go window-shopping
lihat-lihat saja [lihat]

windscreen kaca depan
wine anggur
winery kilang anggur
wings sayap
winner pemenang
winter musim dingin
wire kawat
wise bijaksana
to wish ingin [ingin]
with dengan
within dalam

within an hour
dalam satu jam

without tanpa
without filter tanpa filter
woman orang perempuan/wanita
wonderful bagus sekali
wood (timber) kayu
woodcarving ukiran kayu
wool wol
word kata
work pekerjaan
to work bekerja [kerja]
workout (sport) latihan
work permit izin/visa kerja
workshop ruang kerja
world dunia
World Cup juara dunia
worms cacing
worried kawatir
worship ibadat
worth harga
wound (injury) luka
wristwatch jam tangan
to write menulis [tulis]
writer penulis
writing paper kertas tulis
wrong salah

I'm wrong. (my fault)
Saya salah.

Y

year tahun

this year
tahun ini

yellow kuning
yes ya

yesterday	kemarin
yesterday afternoon kemarin sore yesterday morning kemarin pagi	
yet (not yet)	belum
you	
(inf))	kamu/engkau
(pol)	saudara/Anda
(pl)	kalian
young	muda
youth (collective)	remaja
youth hostel	losmen pemuda

Z

zebra	zebra
zodiac	bintang kelahiran
zoo	kebun binatang

Root words (see Grammar, page 19) are given in brackets after verbs and adjectives. (Root words are often used in conversation by Indonesian speakers.)

melihat [lihat]	to look

Root words also appear as a separate entry, in which case the verb or adjective form is given in brackets after the root.

lihat [melihat]	look

Remember that nouns don't change their form according to whether they're singular or plural.

If you can't find a word in the dictionary, there's a good chance the word is a singkatan, 'abbreviation'.

In this dictionary, when there's a choice between two words, they are separated by a slash:

anggur	grape/wine

A

ABRI (Angkatan Bersenjata Republik Indonesia)	armed forces
abu-abu	grey
acara	program (TV)
ada	there is/are • to be/have/exist

Ada apa?
What's the matter?

adat	custom (tradition)
adik ...	younger ...
laki-laki	brother
perempuan	sister
advokat	lawyer
agama [beragama]	religion
agen (perjalanan)	(travel) agent
ahli	specialist
ahli hukum	lawyer
ahli jamu	herbalist
ahli nujum	fortune teller
air	water
air dingin	cold water
air mata	tear (crying)
air matang	boiled water
air mineral	mineral water
air panas	hot water
air putih	purified water
air terjun	waterfall
akal	sense
akhir [mengakhiri]	end
akhir minggu	weekend
aki	battery

A

aku	I/me/mine
akui [mengakui]	recognise
alam	nature
alamat	address (of house)
alasan	excuse/reason
alat	tool/instrument
alat bantu dengar	hearing aid
alat cukur	razor
alat pemanas	heater
alat pembuka botol	bottle opener
alat pembuka kaleng	can opener
alat selam	diving equipment
Allah	Muslim God
alpukat	avocado
alun-alun	square (in town)
aman	safe (adj)
amatir	amateur
ambil [mengambil]	take
ambruk	collapse
amplop	envelope
anak	child
anak-anak	children
anak anjing	puppy
anak kucing	kitten
anak ...	
laki-laki	boy/son
perempuan	girl/daughter
Anda	you/your
aneh	odd (strange)
anggota	member
anggur	grape/wine
angin	wind
angka	figures
angkot	city transport
anjing	dog
anjing penuntun	guidedog
anjungan tunai mandiri (ATM)	automatic teller machine (ATM)
antara	between
anting-anting	earring
antri	queue
apa	what

Apa artinya?
What does it mean?
Apa itu?
What is that?

apa saja	any (thing)
apakah	question marker

Apakah bis ini ke Kuta?
Does this bus go to Kuta?

apel	apple
api	fire
apokat	avocado
apotik	chemist/pharmacy
arti	meaning
asal [berasal]	come from
asam	sour
asap	a smoke
asbak	ashtray

Asik!
Fantastic!

asin	salty
asing	foreign
asli	indigenous/original
asma	asthma

DICTIONARY

asuransi insurance
atap roof
atau or
atur [mengatur] organise
awan [berawan] cloud
ayah father (biological)
ayam chicken

Ayo!
Come on!

B

babi pig
baca [membaca] read
badai storm
badan body
bagaimana how
bagasi luggage
bagi [membagi] part (divide)
bagian a part
bagian penjualan sales department
bagus great • marvellous • wonderful
bahan baju material (for clothing)
bahasa language
Bahasa Indonesia Indonesian
bahaya dangerous
bahu shoulders
baik good • nice • OK
baik-hati kind (adj)
baju renang bathing suit
bakar burn/roast
balas [membalas] reply
balasan a reply
balita child under the age of five
ban tyre
banci transsexual/transvestite
bandara airport
bangga pride
bangun [membangun] wake up • build
bantah [membantah] argue
bantal pillow
bantu [membantu] assist/help
bantuan assistance
banyak many • much • a lot
bapak dad • father • Mr • sir
bapak mertua father-in-law
bapak tiri stepfather
barang goods (possessions)
barang yang ditinggalkan left luggage
barangkali perhaps
barat west
baru new • just (only now)
basah wet
batal [membatalkan] cancel

batas kecepatan	speed limit
batu	rock/stone
batuk	cough (n/v)
bau	a smell
bawa [membawa]	bring/carry
bawang bombay	onion
bawang putih	garlic
bayangan	reflection (mirror)
bayar [membayar]	pay
bayaran	payment
bayi	baby
bea	rate of pay/ exchange
bea dan cukai	customs (border)
bebas	free (not bound)
bebek	duck
beberapa	few • some • several
bedak bayi	baby powder

Begitu!
It's like that!

belajar	to learn
belanja [berbelanja]	shopping
beli [membeli]	buy
belimbing	starfruit
beliung	pick (axe)
belok (kanan/kiri)	turn (right/left)
belum	not yet
bemo	minibus • public transport
benang	thread
benang gigi	dental floss
benar	right (correct) • true
benda	object
bendera	flag
bengkel	garage
bensin	petrol
bentuk	shape
beracun [racun]	poisonous
beragama	religious
berangkat	depart
berani	brave

Berapa?
How many/much?

beras	rice (uncooked)
berasal [asal]	to come from
berat	heavy/weight
berawan [awan]	to cloud (over)
berbahasa Indonesia	to speak (Indonesian)
berbaring	lay down
berbeda	different
berburu [buru]	to hunt
bercakap [cakap]	to talk/chat
bercanda [canda]	to joke
bercumbu-cumbuan [cumbu]	to chat up
berdarah [darah]	to bleed
berdinas militer	military service
berguna	useful
berharga	valuable

berhenti [henti] to stop
berhutang owe
beri [memberi] give
berita news
berjalan kaki [jalan kaki] to walk/hike
berjoget [joget] to dance
berkata [kata] to say
berkebun [kebun] to garden
berkeliling [keliling] tour • travel around
berkemah [kemah] to camp
berkeringat [keringat] to sweat
bekerja [kerja] to work
berenang [renang] to swim
bermain [main] to play
bersama with/together
bersantai [santai] to relax
berselancar [selancar] to surf
bersih clean
bertanya [tanya] to ask
bertengkar [tengkar] to fight
bertemu [temu] to meet
berteriak [teriak] to shout
beruntung lucky
besar big

besaran size (of anything)
besok tomorrow
besok ... tomorrow ...
  pagi morning
  sore afternoon
betina female (animal)

Betul!
Really! • Sure! • That's right!

biara convent/monastery
biarawan monk
biarawati nun
biasa ordinary/usual
bibi aunt
bibir lips
bicara speak
bijaksana sensible/wise
bilang to say
bilyar pool (game)
binatang animal
binatu laundry
bintang star (in the sky)
bintang kelahiran zodiac
bioskop cinema
bir beer
biru blue
bis ... bus ...
  antar kota intercity
  kota city
  malam night
bisa able/can
bisu mute
bocor leak

bodoh	idiot/stupid
bohong [membohong]	a lie (untruth)
boks telpon	phone box
bola	ball (sport)
bola lampu	light bulb
boleh	it's allowed • may • possible
bon	bill/check
boneka	doll (toy)
bosan	bored
botol (air)	(water) bottle
buah-buahan	fruit
buaian	hammock
buat [membuat]	for/make
buatan	synthetic
buatan tangan	handmade
bujang	single (male)
buka [membuka]	open
bukan	no/not

Bukan main!
No joke!

bukit	hill
buku	book
buku catatan	notebook
buku doa	prayer book
buku pedoman	guidebook
buku perjalanan	travel (books)
buku telpon	phone book
bulan	month/moon
bulat	round (shape)
bule	westerner (col)
bumi	earth
buncis	beans
bundaran	roundabout
bunga	flower
bungkus	packet/container
bunuh [membunuh]	kill
bunyi	noise • ring (of phone)
bupati	head of regency
buru [berburu]	hunt
buruk	bad
buruk sekali	terrible
burung	bird
busuk	stale/rotten
buta	blind (no vision)

C

cabang	branch (office)
cabe	chilli
cacat	faulty/disabled
cacat kaki	paraplegic
cacing	worms
cairan	lotion
cakap [bercakap]	chat/talk
camat	head of a district
campur	mix
canda [bercanda]	joke
candi	Buddhist temple
cangkir	cup
cantik	beautiful/pretty
cari [mencari]	search
cat [mencat]	paint
catatan harian	diary

catur	chess
cek (turis)	(travellers) cheque(s)
celana dalam	underwear
celana panjang	trousers
celana pendek	shorts (clothes)
cemara	fir/pine
cengkeh	clove
cepat	fast/quick
cerah	sunny/light
cerai	divorce
cerdik	crafty
cerita	story
cerita pendek	short story
cermin	mirror
cetakan	a print (artwork)
cincin	ring (on finger)
cinta	love
cium [mencium]	kiss/smell
coba [mencoba]	attempt
cocok	appropriate
coklat	brown/chocolate
contoh	example
copet	pickpocket
cuaca	weather
cuci [mencuci]	wash/develop
cucu	grandchild
cukup	enough
cukur	shave
cumbu [bercumbu-cumbuan]	chat
curam	steep (hill)
curi [mencuri]	steal

D

Daag.
Goodbye. (inf)

dada	chest (body)
dadu	dice/die
daerah	regional
daerah luar kota	countryside
daftar makanan	menu
daftar waktu	timetable
daging	meat
daging babi	ham/pork
daging domba	mutton
daging sapi	beef
dalam	deep • in • within
damai	peace
dan	and
danau	lake
dandanan	make-up (cosmetics)
dangdut	style of Indonesian music (see page 99)
dapat [mendapat]	to earn/obtain
dapur	kitchen
darah [berdarah]	blood
darah rendah/tinggi	low/high blood pressure
dari	from
dari mana	from where
darurat	emergency
datang	to come/arrive
datar	flat
dataran tinggi	plateau

daur ulang — recycle/recycling
debu — dust
dekat — near
demam — temperature (fever)
demam tipus — typhoid
demo — rally (demonstration)
denda — a payable fine
dengan — with
dengar [mendengar] — hear
depan — front
derita [menderita] — suffer
desa — village
detik — second (unit of time)
dewasa — adult
di — at/on
dia — s/he
di antara — among/between
diare — diarrhoea
di atas — aboard/above
di bawah — under/below
di belakang — at the back
dibuat (dari) — made (of)
di dalam — inside
di depan — ahead • in front of
dilarang — forbidden
dilarang masuk — no entry
dilarang merokok — no smoking
di mana — where
di mana saja — anywhere
dinas — official (of government)
dinding — wall (inside)
dingin — cold

Dirgahayu ...!
Long live ...!

di samping — beside • next to
di sana — (over) there
di seberang (dinding) — over (the wall)
di sini — (over) here
di situ — there (nearby)
ditinggalkan — to be left (behind or over)
doa — prayer
dokter gigi — dentist
domba — sheep
dompet — wallet/purse
dorong [mendorong] — push
dosa — sin
dosen — lecturer
dot — dummy/pacifier
DPR (Dewan Perwakilan Rakyat) — Indonesian Legislative Assembly
dua-duanya — both
dua kali — twice
duduk — sit
duit — cash/banknotes
dulu — past (before) • first
dunia — earth/world
duta besar — ambassador

E

egois — selfish
ekor — tail (of an animal)
emas — gold

ember — bucket
enak — delicious/tasty
encok — rheumatism
engkau — you/your
es — ice

F

filem — film (camera) • movie

G

gading — ivory
gaji — salary
gambar — picture
Gamelan — type of Indonesian music
gang — alley
ganggu [mengganggu] — annoy
gangguan — harassment
ganja — dope • hashish • marijuana
ganjil — odd (number)
ganteng — handsome (m)
ganti [mengganti] — change
garam — salt
garis — line
garpu — fork
gatal — itch/horny
gay — gay/homosexual
gaya — style
gedung — building
gelap — dark
gelas — glass
gelinding — rolling
gelisah — nervous
gembira — happy
gempa bumi — earthquake
gemuk — fat (adj)
gendang — drums
genit — sleazy (person)
gerbong — van
gereja — church
gigit — teeth
gigit [mengigit] — bite
gigitan — bite (of dog/insect)
gila — crazy • delirious • mad
gincu — lipstick
goa — cave
golongan darah — blood group
goreng — fried
gratis — free (of charge)
gua — cave
gubernur — head of province
gula — sugar
gunting — scissors
gunung — mountain
gunung api — volcano
gurih — rich (food)
guru — teacher
gurun pasir — desert

H

habis — finished
hadiah — gift
hak asasi manusia (HAM) — human rights

hakim	judge (head of court)
hak yang sama	equal opportunity
halaman	page (of book) • sheet (of paper) • yard (of house)
hama	bug (animal)
hamil	pregnant
hampir	almost
handuk	towel
hangat	warm
hanya	only
harga	cost/price/worth
hari	day
hari ini	today
Hari Jumat	Friday
Hari Kamis	Thursday
Hari Minggu	Sunday
Hari Natal	Christmas
Hari Proklamasi Kemedekaan	Independence Day (August 17)
Hari Rabu	Wednesday
Hari Sabtu	Saturday
Hari Selasa	Tuesday
Hari Senin	Monday
Hari Tahun Baru	New Year's Day
hari ulang tahun	birthday
harian	daily
harimau	tiger
harus	must
hasil	result
hati	liver

Hati-hati!
Careful! • Watch out!

haus	thirsty
hebat	intense
helm	helmet
henti [berhenti]	stop
hibur [menghibur]	entertain
hidung	nose
hidup	life • alive • to live
hijau	green
hilang	to lose (something)
hitam	black
hitung [menghitung]	count
homoseks	gay/homosexual
hormat	respect

hotel murah
cheap hotel

hubungan	relationship
hujan	rain
hujan deras	heavy rain
hukum	law
hukuman	penalty/sentence
hutan	forest

I

ialah	to be
ibadat	worship
ibu	mother/Mrs
ibu mertua	mother-in-law
ibu tiri	step mother
ide	idea

Idul Adha	Feast of the Sacrifice (Muslim festival)
ikan	a fish
iklan	advertisement
ikut [mengikuti]	follow
ilmu bumi	geography
ilmu sosial	social sciences
ilmuwan	scientist
imbang [mengimbangkan]	to balance
inap [menginap]	stay
indah	beautiful (scenery or garden)
ingat	remember
Inggris	English
ingin	to wish
ini	thi
insinyur	engineer
interlokal	long distance
irama	rhythm
iri hati	jealous
iris [mengiris]	slice
isi [mengisi]	fill
istana	palace
istimewa	special
istirahat	rest/intermission
istri	wife
itu	that
izin	permission/permit
izin masuk	permission to enter

J

jadwal	timetable
jahat	bad (eg attitude)
jahit	sew
jaipongan	Indonesian dance (see page 104)
jala	net
jalan	road • street • trail • route • way
jalan [menjalankan]	to drive
jalan-jalan	stroll • walk • to travel
jalan kaki [berjalan kaki]	walk/hike
jalan kecil	track • path • footpath
jalan masuk	entrance
jalan raya	avenue • main road
jalan tol	motorway (tollway)
jam	clock/hour

Jam berapa?
What time is it?

jam tangan	wristwatch
jam weker	alarm clock
jaminan sosial	social security
jamu	herbal medicine • mushroom

Jangan repot.
Don't trouble yourself.

janji	appointment • date • engagement • promise
jantung	heart
jantan	male (animal)
jarak	distance (in length)
jarang	rare (not common)
jari	finger
jarum	needle (sewing)
jarum suntik	syringe
jas	coat
jasa	service (assistance)
jatuh	drop • to collapse
jauh	far
jawab [menjawab]	answer
jejak	track (footprints)
jelas	clear • understood • obvious
jelek	bad
jembatan	bridge
jemur (menjemur)	dry
jendela	window
jengkerik	cricket (animal)
jenis	type (of product)
jeruk	orange (food)
jeruk nipis	lemon
jilbab	Muslim head scarf
jingga	orange (colour)
jip	jeep
joget [berjoget]	dance
jual	sell
juara dunia	World Cup
juga	also • too (as well)
jumlah	quantity
jurang	ledge/cliff
jururawat	nurse
jus	juice
juta	million

K

kabut	fog
kaca	glass/mirror
kaca depan	windscreen
kaca mata	glasses (eye)
kaca mata hitam	sunglasses
kacang	nut (food)
kacapi suling	Indonesian music (see page 102)
kacau	disorder/uproar
kadang-kadang	sometimes
kado	present (gift)
kagum (mengagumi)	admire
kakak ... laki-laki / perempuan	older ... brother / sister
kakek	grandfather
kaki	foot/leg
kaku	stiff/rigid
kalah	loss
kalau	if
kaleng	can/tin
kali	stream (small river)
kalian	you (pl)
kalimat	sentence (words)
kalung	necklace
kamar	room
kamar kecil	toilet

DICTIONARY

kamar mandi	bathroom
kamar tidur	bedroom
kambing	goat
kami	we (excluding listener – see page 24)
kampung	village
kamu	you/your
kamus	dictionary
kanan	right (not left)
kancing	buttons
kantor	office
kantor pariwisata	tourist information office
kantor pos	post office
kantor telpon	telephone office
kantung	pocket
kaos kaki	socks
kapal	ship
kapan saja	anytime

Kapan?
When?

karantina	quarantine
karcis	ticket
karena	because
kartu kredit	credit card
kartu nama	card (name)
kartu (main)	playing cards
kartu pos	postcard
kartu telpon	phonecard
kartun	cartoons
karyawan	worker/employee
kasar	vulgar
kasih	love
kasir	teller/cashier
kassa	teller/cashier
kasur	mattress
kata [berkata]	word • say
katun	cotton
kau	you (sg, inf); short for engkau
kawan	companion
kawat	telegram/wire
kawatir	worry/worried
kawin	marry
kaya	rich (wealthy)
kayu	wood (timber)
ke	to
ke arah	towards (direction)
keadilan	justice
keahlian teknik	engineering
kebangsaan	nationality
kebenaran	truth
keberangkatan	departure
kebiasaan	habit
kebocoran	puncture
kebun [berkebun]	garden
kebun binatang	zoo
kebun raya	botanical gardens
kecanduan	addiction
kecap asin	soy sauce
kecelakaan	accident
kecepatan	speed
kecil	little/small
kedatangan	arrivals
kedua	second (in order)
keduanya	both
kedutaan besar	embassy
kegemaran	hobby
keguguran	miscarriage

K

keheranan	surprise
keju	cheese
kejuaraan	championship
kekasih	lover
kekuatan	strength
kekurangan	shortage
kelambu	mosquito net
kelapa	coconut
kelas	class
kelenteng	Chinese temple
kelinci	rabbit
kelompok	group
keluar	exit
keluarga	family
keluhan	complaint
kemah [berkemah]	camp

Ke mana?
To where?

kemarin	yesterday
kemarin dulu	day before yesterday
kemarin pagi/sore	yesterday morning/ afternoon
kematian	death

kembali
You're welcome. • return

kembar	twins
kemeja	shirt
kemiskinan	poverty
kemungkinan	chance
kenal	to know (someone)

Kenapa?
Why?

kencing	urine
kencing manis	diabetes
kenek	ticket collector
kentang	potato
kentut	fart
kenyang	full (of food)
kepala	head
kepala desa/ kampung	head of a village
kepala stasiun	station master
kepanasan	heat • to be hot
kepiting	crab
kepribadian	personality
kepur-bakalaan	archaeological
kerajinan tangan	handicrafts
keramah-tamahan	hospitality
keramas	to shampoo
kerang	shell (sea)
keranjang	basket
keras	hard/loud
keras kepala	stubborn
keren	cool (col)
kereta api	train
kereta makan	dining car
kereta tidur	sleeping car
kering	dry (adj)
keringat [berkeringat]	sweat
kerja [bekerja]	work
kertas	paper
kertas kloset	toilet paper
kerugian	disadvantage

Indonesian	English
kesehatan	health
kesejahteraan	welfare
keseleo	a sprain
kesempatan	chance
kesepuluh	tenth
ketakutan	fear
ketegangan sebelum menstruasi	premenstrual tension
keterangan	information
ketidaksamaan	inequality
ketik [mengetik]	type
ketimun	cucumber
ketinggian	altitude
keturunan	descendent
kewarga-negaraan	citizenship
khas	typical
khayal [menghayalkan]	hallucinate
kidal	left-handed
kijang	deer
kilang anggur	winery
kina	quinine
kios	kiosk
kios telpon	phone office
kipas (tangan)	fan (hand-held)
kiper	goalkeeper
kira-kira	approximately
kiri	left (not right)
Kiri!	Stop!
kirim [mengirim]	send
kita	we (including the listener – see page 24)
Kitab	the Bible
klub (malam)	(night)club
kode pos	postcode
kodok	frog/toad
kokain	cocaine
kol	cabbage
kolam renang	swimming pool
kompor	stove
komuni	communion
kontan	cash/banknotes
kopi	coffee
kopor	suitcase
koran	newspaper
korek api	matches
korting	discount
kosong	empty/vacant
kost	share accommodation
kota	city
kotak	box (package)
kotak pertolongan pertama	first-aid kit
kotak pos	mailbox
kotor	dirty
kotoran	faeces
kretek	clove cigarettes
krim pelembab	moisturising cream
krim penahan matahari	sunblock
KTP (Kartu Tanda Penduduk)	identification card

K

DICTIONARY

kuasa	power
kuat	strong
kuburan	grave
kucing	cat
kuda	horse
kue	cake
kuliah	lecture
kulit	leather/skin
kulkas	refrigerator
kumpulan tetap	permanent collection
kunci [mengunci]	key/lock
kuning	yellow
kunjung [mengunjungi]	visit
kuno	ancient • old-fashioned
kupu-kupu	butterfly/prostitute
kupu-kupu malam	prostitute
kura-kura	turtle
kurang	less
kurs	rate of pay/ exchange
kursi	chair/seat
kursi roda	wheelchair
kurus	skinny
kutu	flea/lice
kwitansi	receipt

L

lada	pepper
ladang	field
lagi	again
lagu	song
lain	other

Lain kali.
Next time.

laki-laki	male
laku [melakukan]	do
lalat	fly
lalu-lintas	traffic
lama	long (time) • old (building)
lampu	light/lamp
lampu lalu-lintas/merah	traffic lights
lancar	fluent
langit	sky
langkah	step
langsung	direct
lantai	floor
lapangan	square (in town)
lapangan tenis	tennis court
lapangan terbang	airport
lapangan udara	airport
lapar	hungry
lapor [melaporkan]	report
lari	run
lari lintas alam	cross-country trail
latihan	exercise
laut	ocean/sea
lawan	opposite
layar	sail • screen (film)
lebar	wide

Lebaran (Idul Fitri)	end of Ramadan
lebih	more
lebih baik	better
lekas	early
lelah	tired
lelucon	joke
lem	glue
lemah	weak
lemari	wardrobe
lemari es	refrigerator
lembab	humid
lembah	valley
lembut	gentle/soft
lengan	arm
lesbi	lesbian
liburan	holiday/vacation
lidah	tongue
lihat [melihat]	look
lihat-lihat	to look around
lilin	candle
lindung [melindungi]	protect
lingkungan	environment
lisan	oral
listrik	electricity
lobang	hole
logam	metal
loket	ticket office/ window
lompat	jump (across)
loncat	jump (high)
longgar	loose
losmen	hotel
losmen pemuda	youth hostel
luar	outside
luar biasa	unusual
luar negri	abroad
luas	large
lucu	cute (baby) • funny
luka	wound/injury
luka memar	bruise
lukis [melukis]	paint
lukisan	paintings
lumpur	mud
lupa	forget
lurus	straight
lusa	day after tomorrow
lusin	a dozen
lutut	knee
luwes	charming

M

ma'af [mema'afkan]	sorry
mabuk	stoned/drunk
mabuk jalan	travel sick
mabuk laut	seasick
macam	type (of product)
macet	traffic jam
madu	honey
mahal	expensive
mahasiswa	student (university)
main [bermain]	play
mainan	game
majalah	magazine
majikan	employer
makan	eat
makan malam	dinner
makan pagi	breakfast
makan siang	lunch

makanan	food
makanan untuk bayi	baby food
makna	meaning
malam	evening/night
Malam Natal	Christmas Eve
Malam Tahun Baru	New Year's Eve
malam ini	tonight

malam minggu
Saturday night

malas	lazy
maling	thief
malu	ashamed/shy/embarrassed
mandi	bath • to bathe/wash
mangga	mango
manis	sweet (adj)
mantel	overcoat
marah	angry
mari	goodbye (inf)
marmot	guinea pig
masa depan	future
masak	to cook

Masak?
Really? • Is that so?

masalah	problem
masih	still/presently

Masih pagi-pagi.
It's early.

masing-masing	every/each
masuk	enter/entrance
masuk angin	to have the flu
masyarakat	society
mata	eye
matahari	sun
matahari terbenam	sunset
matahari terbit	sunrise
matang	ripe
mati	die
mau	to want
mayoritas	majority
Mbak	Miss (used for a female younger than you)
meja	table
melawan	against (opposed)
melukis [lukis]	painting (the art)
melakukan [laku]	to do
melaporkan [lapor]	to report
melindungi [lindung]	to protect
melukis [lukis]	to paint
mema'afkan [ma'af]	to forgive
memakai [pakai]	to wear
memalukan [malu]	embarrassing
memancing	to fish
memastikan [pasti]	to confirm
membaca [baca]	to read
membagi [bagi]	to part (divide)

membalas [balas] to reply
membangun [bangun] to build • to wake up
membantah [bantah] to argue
membantu [bantu] to assist
membatalkan [batal] to cancel
membawa [bawa] to bring/carry
membayangkan to imagine
membayar [bayar] to pay
membeli [beli] to buy
memberi [beri] to give
memberikan suara to vote
membersihkan [bersih] to clean
membohongi [bohong] to tell a lie
membolehkan [boleh] to allow
membosankan [bosan] boring
membuat [buat] to make
membuat angka to score
membuka [buka] to open
membunuh [bunuh] to kill
memelihara [pelihara] to protect
memeluk cuddle
memeriksa [periksa] to examine
memesan [pesan] to book • to reserve • to order
memijit [pijit] to massage
memikirkan [pikir] to think
memilih [pilih] to choose
meminjam [pinjam] to borrow
meminjankan [pinjam] to lend
memisahkan [pisah] to separate
memotong [potong] to cut
memperlihatkan [lihat] to exhibit
memperolok-olokkan [olok] to make fun of
memungut [pungut] to pick something up
memutuskan [putus] to decide
menang win
menara tower
menari [tari] to dance
menarik interesting
menasehati [nasehat] to advise
mencari [cari] to search
mencat [cat] to paint
mencium [cium] to kiss/smell

M

mencoba [coba] — to attempt
mencret — diarrhoea
mencuci [cuci] — to wash/develop
mencuri [curi] — to steal
mendaki — to scale/climb
mendaki gunung — mountaineering
mendapat [dapat] — to earn/obtain
mendayung — rowing
mendengar [dengar] — to hear
menderita [derita] — to suffer
mendidik — to educate
mendorong [dorong] — to push
mendung — cloudy
menelpon [telpon] — to telephone
menemani [teman] — to accompany
menembak [tembak] — to shoot
menemukan [temu] — to discover/find
mengagumi [kagum] — to admire
mengajar — teaching
mengakhiri [akhir] — to end
mengakui [akui] — to acknowledge/recognise
mengambil [ambil] — to take

Mengapa?
Why?

mengatur [atur] — to organise
mengeluh — to complain
mengerikan — horrible
mengerti — to understand
mengetik [ketik] — to type
mengganggu [ganggu] — to annoy
mengganti [ganti] — to change
menggonceng — to hitchhike
menghayalkan [khayal] — to hallucinate
menghibur [hibur] — to entertain
menghitung [hitung] — to count
menggigit [gigit] — to bite
mengikuti [ikut] — to follow/join
menginap [inap] — to stay overnight
mengirim [kirim] — to send
mengiris [iris] — to slice
mengisi [isi] — to fill
mengucapkan [ucap] — to express
mengulangi [ulang] — to repeat
mengunci [kunci] — to lock
mengunjungi [kunjung] — to visit

menanam [tanam]	to plant
menandatangani [tandatangan]	to sign
menerima [terima]	to accept
menerjemahkan [terjemah]	to translate
menikah [nikah]	to marry
menikmati [nikmat]	to enjoy yourself
menimbang [timbang]	to weigh
meninggal	to die (person) • dead (person)
menit	minute
menitipkan [titip]	to deposit (luggage)
menjaga anak	childminding
menjalankan [jalan]	to drive
menjawab [jawab]	to answer
menjemur [jemur]	to dry
menolak [tolak]	to refuse
menolong [tolong]	to help
menonton [tonton]	to watch
menstruasi	menstruation
mentah	raw/unripe
mentega	butter
menukarkan [tukar]	to exchange
menulis [tulis]	to write
menunggu [tunggu]	to wait
menunjuk [tunjuk]	to show
menutup [tutup]	to close
menyadari [sadar]	to realise
menyakitkan	painful
menyangkal [sangkal]	to deny
menyanyi [nyanyi]	to sing
menyelam [selam]	to dive
menyelamatkan [selamat]	to save
menyentuh [sentuh]	to touch
menyesal [sesal]	to regret
menyewa [sewa]	to rent
menyiapkan [siap]	to prepare
menyiksa [siksa]	to punish
menyimpan [simpan]	to put
menyinggung perasaan	offence (personal)
menyogok [sogok]	to bribe

menyuntikkan [suntik] to inject
menyusahkan pain in the neck
merah red
merah muda pink
Merah Putih Red & White (the Indonesian flag)
merampok [rampok] to rob
merasa [rasa] to feel
merayakan [raya] to celebrate
merdeka free/independent
mereka they
merica pepper
merokok [rokok] to smoke
merusakkan [rusak] to destroy
mesin engine/machine
mesin cuci washing machine
mesjid mosque
meteran lampu light meter
mewah luxury
mie noodles
mimpi to dream
minggu week
minggu ini this week

Minta!
May I? • Could I please?

minum to drink
minuman drink (n)
minyak oil (cooking)
mirip similar
misa religious service
misalnya for example
miskin poor
mobil car
mogok broken down • on strike
montir mechanic
monyet monkey
mu you (sg, inf); short for **kamu**
mual nausea
muda young
mudah easy
muka face
mulai begin
mulut mouth
mungkin maybe • perhaps • possibly
muntah vomit (n/v)
murah cheap
murah hati generous
murid student (school)
murni pure
musim season
musim bunga spring (season)
musim dingin winter
musim gugur autumn (fall)
musim panas summer
musim semi spring (season)
musium museum

N

naik to board • to ride • to take (the train) • up • uphill
nama name
nama keluarga surname

nama panggilan	nickname
nanas	pineapple
nangka	jackfruit
nanti	later
napas	breath
nasehat [menasehati]	advice
nasi	rice (cooked)
naskah	script
negara	country
nenek	grandmother
ngantuk	sleepy
nikah [menikah]	marry
nikmat [menikmati]	enjoy
nilai	value (price)
nomor	number
nomor kamar	room number
nomor paspor	passport number
nyaman	comfortable
nyamuk	mosquito
nyanyi [menyanyi]	sing
Nyepi	Hindu New Year

O

obat	medicine/drugs
obat sakit kepala	aspirin
obat pencahar	laxatives
obat tidur	sleeping pills
obral	on sale
odol	toothpaste
olahraga	sport
olahragawan	sportsman
olahragawati	sportswoman
oleh-oleh	souvenir
oli	oil (crude)
ombak	waves
ongkos	price (of a service)
orang	person
orang asing	foreigner
orang gaya	trendy (person)
orang jalanan	homeless
orang minta-minta	beggar
orang-orang	people
orang suci	saint
orang tua	parents
oranye	orange (colour)
otak	brain
otot	muscle

P

pabean	customs (border)
pabrik	factory
pacar (laki-laki/ perempuan)	boyfriend/ girlfriend
pada	at (time)

pada siang/sore
in the afternoon

padat	solid
pagar	fence
pagi	morning
pagi-pagi	early

Paham.
I understand.

pajak	tax

O

DICTIONARY

P

pakai [memakai]	to use/wear
pakaian	clothing
paket	parcel
paling	most
paling baik	best
palu	hammer
pameran	exhibition
panas	hot
panci	pot (cooking)
panggang	roasted
panggung	stage
panjang	length/long
pantai	beach/coast
papan	a board
papan selancar	surfboard
papaya	pawpaw
parkir	carpark
parlamen	parliament
partai	party (politics)
pas	a pass
pas naik	boarding pass
pasang	tide
pasar ...	... market
malam	night
swalayan	super
pasir	sand
Paskah	Easter
paspor	passport
pasta gigi	toothpaste
pasti [memastikan]	confirm
patah	broken
patung	statue
payung	umbrella
pecah	break/puncture
pecandu	addict/addiction
pedagang narkotika	drug dealer
pedang	sword
pedas	spicy
pegawai bank	bank clerk
pegunungan	mountain range
pejalan kaki	pedestrian
pekerja	worker/employee
pekerja bebas	self-employed
pekerjaan	job • occupation • work
pelabuhan	harbour/port
pelajar	student (school)
pelan	slow
pelanggaran	offense (legal)
pelatih	instructor
pelaut	sailor
pelawak	clown
pelayan	waiter
pelayanan	service
pelayanan sendiri	self-service
pelihara [memelihara]	protect
pelor gas	gas cartridge
pelosok	remote
peluk	hug
pelukis	painter (artist)
pemain musik	musician
pemakaman	funeral
pemandangan	scenery/view
pemandu	guide
pembakaran mayat	cremation
pembalut	bandage

pembantu servant
pembersihan cleaning
pembohong liar
pembuatan construction work
pembuka opener
pemerintah government
pemikiran reflection (thinking)
pemilihan umum elections
pemilik owner
pemilu elections
pemimpin leader/manager
pemungut karcis ticket collector
pena pen
penangkal infeksi antiseptic
penawar sakit painkillers
pencacaran vaccination
pencocok adaptor (electric)
pendaftaran mobil car registration
pendapat opinion
pendek short (length or height)
pendeta priest
pendidikan education
penebangan hutan deforestation
penegasan confirmation
penerbangan flight
pengadilan court (legal)
pengakuan confession (religious)
pengalaman experience
pengambilan barang baggage claim
penganggur unemployed
penganut Buda Buddhist
pengesahan endorsement
penggemar fan (of a team)
penghasil producer
penghubung (telpon) (telephone) operator
penginapan accommodation
pengunduran diri resignation
pengungsi refugee
pengusaha business person
penipu cheat
penjaga anak babysitter
penjahit tailor
penjara prison
penjual seller
pensiun pensioner/retired
penting important/urgent
penuh full
penukaran exchange
penulis writer
penumpang passenger
penunjuk indicator
penyakit sickness/disease
penyakit kelamin venereal disease
penyanyi singer
penyiar presenter (TV, etc)
per spring (coil)
perahu boat
perahu motor motorboat
perak silver
peralatan equipment
perang war
perangko postage/stamp

perasaan	feelings
peraturan	rules
perayaan	celebration/ festival
perban	bandage
perbatasan	border
percaya	to trust/believe
percintaan	romance
perdana menteri	prime minister
perempat	quarter
perempatan	crossroad
perempuan	woman
pergi	to go

Pergi!
Get lost!

perguruan tinggi	college
perhiasan	jewellery
periksa [memeriksa]	to check/examine
periksa darah	blood test
perincian	detail
perjalanan	journey/trip
perjalanan kaki	trek
perkawinan	marriage
perkebunan	farm
perkosaan	rape
perlombaan	race (sport)
perlu	essential • need • necessary
permadani	rug
permen	sweets
permen karet	chewing gum
permisi	excuse me
pernikahan	marriage
peron	platform
perpustakaan	library
persamaan	equality
persegi	square (shape)
persimpangan	intersection
pertama	first
pertandingan	game/match
Pertandingan Olympiade	Olympic Games
pertanian	agriculture/farm
pertanyaan	question
pertemuan	meeting
pertengkaran	fight/quarrel
pertunangan	engagement (wedding)
pertunjukan	show/ performance
perundang-undangan	legislation
perusahaan	company (business)
perut	stomach
pesan [memesan]	order/message
pesanan tempat	reservation
pesawat terbang	plane
pesawat udara	aeroplane
pesta	party
peta	map
petani	farmer
peti besi	a safe
pidato	speech
pijit [memijit]	massage

pikir [memikirkan] — think
pikiran — thought
pil kontrasepsi — the Pill
pilek — cold (head)
pilih [memilih] — choose
pinggir — side (of a street)
pinggir kota — suburb
pingsan — to faint
pinjam [meminjam] — borrow
pintu — door/gate
pintu masuk — entrance
pipa — pipe (plumbing)
piring — plate
pisah [memisahkan] — separate
pisang — banana
pisau — knife
plakat — poster
pohon — tree
polisi — police
politikus — politicians
pompa — pump
pondok — mountain hut
ponsel — mobile phone
popok — nappy
pos — mail/post
pos kamling — neighbourhood security post
pos kilat — express mail
pos pemeriksaan — checkpoint
pos tercatat — registered mail
pos udara — airmail
potong [memotong] — piece
pranama — first name
pria — man
pribadi — private
privatisasi — privatisation
puas — content (happy)
puasa — a fast • to fast
puisi — poetry
pulang — to go home
pulang-pergi — return (ticket)
pulau — island
puncak — peak (mountain)
punggung — back (of body)
pungut [memungut] — pick up
punya — to have
pura — Hindu temple
pusing — dizzy
Puskesmas — local government health clinic
putih — white
putus [memutuskan] — decide

R

racun [beracun] — poison
raja — king
rak — shelves
raksasa — giant
rakyat — people
Ramadan — Muslim fasting month
ramah tamah — outgoing • friendly • hospitable

ramai	crowded/busy (place or party)
rambut	hair
rampok [merampok]	rob
ransel	backpack/ knapsack
rapat	meeting
ras	race (breed)
rasa [merasa]	taste/feel
ratu	queen
raya [merayakan]	celebrate
rebus	boil
recehan	loose change
redaktur	editor
regu	team (sport)
rekam	recording
rekan	colleague
rekening	bill (to pay)
remaja	youth
renang [berenang]	swim
rencana	plan
rencana perjalanan	itinerary
renda	lace
rendah	low
resep	prescription
ribut	noisy
rindu	to miss (feel absence)
ringan	light (adj)
risiko	risk
riwayat hidup	resumé
roda	wheel
rok	dress (clothing)
rokok [merokok]	cigarettes
roman	novel (book)
roti	bread
roti bakar	toast (bread)
ruam	rash
ruang	cabin/room
ruang tamu	lounge room
rugi	loss
rumah	house
rumah makan	restaurant
rumah sakit	hospital
rumput	grass
runtuhan	ruins
rusak [merusakkan]	destroy

S

sabar	patient (adj)
sabuk pengaman	seat belt
sabun	soap
sadar [menyadari]	realise
sains	science
sakit	ill • sick • pain
sakit gigi	toothache
sakit kepala	headache
sakit menstruasi	period pain
sakit perut	stomachache
sakit selesma	cold (head)

Salam.
Hello.

salah	fault • mistake • wrong

DICTIONARY

salah cerna — indigestion
salah paham — misunderstanding
salib — cross (religious)
sama — same
sama-sama — together

Sama-sama.
You're welcome.

sampah — garbage/rubbish
sampai (Juni) — until (June)

Sampai jumpa.
See you later.

sampanye — champagne
sandiwara — play (theatre)
sangat — very
sangkal [menyangkal] — deny
santai [bersantai] — relax
sapi — cow
sapu — broom
saring — filtered
sarung bantal — pillowcase
satpam (satuan pengamanan) — security guard
satu arah — one way
satu jalan — one-way (ticket)
satu kali — once
satu saja — just one
saudara — you/your
saya — I • me • mine

Saya (tidak) mengerti.
I (don't) understand.
Saya Chris.
I'm Chris.
Saya lupa.
I forget.
Saya punya ...
I have ...
Saya salah.
I'm wrong. (my fault)
Saya tidak tahu.
I don't know.

sayang — love
sayap — wings
sayap kanan — right-wing
sayap kiri — left-wing
sayur-sayuran — vegetables
SD (Sekolah Dasar) — elementary school
sebab — because
sebelum — before
sebenarnya — actually

Sebentar.
Just a minute.

seberang — across

sebulan yang lalu
last month

sedang — while/currently
sederhana — plain/simple
sedih — sad
sedikit — a little (amount)
segalanya — everything
segar — fresh
segera — immediately • right now • soon
sehat — well/healthy

S

sejak	since
sejarah	history

Sekakmat
Checkmate!

sekali	once
sekali lagi	once again
sekarang	now
sekolah	school
Sekolah Dasar (SD)	elementary school
seks	sex
selalu	always
selam [menyelam]	dive
selama	during • for (length of time)
selama-lamanya	forever
selamat [menyelamatkan]	safe/save

Selamat datang.
Welcome.
Selamat hari ulang tahun!
Happy birthday!
Selamat jalan.
Goodbye. (when staying) • Happy travels.
Selamat malam.
Good evening/night.
Selamat pagi.
Good morning.
Selamat sore.
Good afternoon.
Selamat tinggal.
Goodbye. (when leaving)
Selamat!
Congratulations!; Cheers! • Good luck!

selancar [berselancar]	surf
selatan	south
selendang	large scarf used as carrier
selimut	blanket
seluruh	whole (all)
semangka	watermelon
sembahyang	prayer
semesta alam	universe

seminggu yang lalu
last week

sempit	tight
sempurna	perfect
semua	all
semua orang	everybody
semut	ant
senang	fun • glad • happy
sendirian	alone
sendok	spoon
seni	art
seni drama	drama
seni ukir	sculpture
seniman	artist
senter	torch (flashlight)
sentuh [menyentuh]	touch
senyum [tersenyum]	smile
sepak bola	football (soccer)
sepasang	pair (a couple)
sepatu	shoes
sepeda	bicycle
sepeda motor	motorcycle
sepi	quiet/calm
seprei	sheet (bed)

DICTIONARY

serangan assault
serangga insect/bug
seratus a hundred
serbet napkin
serbuk sari pollen
seri series
serikat buruh trade union
serikat sekerja unions
sering often
sesal [menyesal] regret
seseorang somebody • someone • a person
sesuatu something
sesudah after
setahun yang lalu one year ago
seteker light/switch/plug
setelah after
setengah half

setengah jam
half an hour

setia loyal
setiap hari every day
setuju agree
sewa [menyewa] hire/rent
siang midday • early afternoon
siap [menyiapkan] ready
siapa who

Siapa ini?
Who is it?

Siapa nama Anda?
What's your name?

sibuk busy (time/schedule)
sikat gigi toothbrush
sikat rambut hairbrush
siksa [menyiksa] to punish
silakan please
silet razor blade
SIM (Surat Izin Mengemudi) drivers licence
simpan [menyimpan] put
simpatik sympathetic
sinetron soap opera
singkatan abbreviation
sirup cordial
sisa rest (what's left)
sisa buangan toksik toxic waste
sisi side
sisir comb
sistem golongan class system
SMA (Sekolah Menengah Atas) upper secondary school
SMP (Sekolah Menengah Pertama) lower secondary school
sogok me-[nyogok] bribe
sore late afternoon
stasiun station/terminal
stasiun kereta railway station
stopan bis bus stop

suami	husband
suara	voice • volume • sound
suasana	atmosphere (of a place)
subuh	dawn (sunrise)
sudah	already
sudut	corner
suhu udara	temperature (weather)
suka	to like
sukar	difficult
sukar buang air	to be constipated
sundal	prostitute
sungai	river
suntik [menyuntikkan]	syringe/injection
surat	letter
surat keterangan	identification/ certificate
surat lahir	birth certificate
surat wesel	bankdraft
susah	difficult
susu	milk
sutra	silk
sutradara	director (of film)
swasta	private
syahwat	orgasm
syal	scarf
sampo	shampoo

T

tadi (malam)	last (night)
tahu	to know (something) • tofu
tahun	year
takut	afraid
tali	string
tali sepatu	shoelaces
taman (nasional)	(national) park
taman kanak-kanak	kindergarten
tambah	plus
tambang	rope/mining
tampan	handsome (male)
tamu	guest
tanah	earth • soil • ground • land

Tanah Air
Land and Water (the nation)

tanam [menanam]	plant
tanaman	a plant
tanda	sign
tandatangan [menandatangani]	signature
tanduk	horn (of animal)
tangan	hand
tangga	stairs/stairway
tanggal	date
tanggal kelahiran	date of birth
tanggung jawab	responsibility
tanpa	without
tante	aunt
tanya [bertanya]	ask
taraf	leg (in race)
tari [menari]	dance

tarif	rate of pay/ exchange
tarik	pull
taruhan	bet/gamble
tas	bag
tas tangan	handbag
tas tidur	sleeping bag
tatabahasa	grammar
tawaran	offer
tawar menawar	to bargain
tebal	thick
teduh	shade
teh	tea
tekanan	pressure
tekanan darah	blood pressure
teks	subtitles
telanjang	nude
telinga	ear
telpon [menelpon]	telephone
telur	egg
teman	friend
tembak [menembak]	shoot
tembakau	tobacco
tembikar	pottery
tembok	wall (outside)
tempat	location • place • space • area
tempat duduk	seat/chair
tempat kelahiran	place of birth
tempat men-daftarkan diri	check-in (desk)
tempat suci	shrine
tempat tenda	campsite
tempat tidur	bed
tempat tujuan	destination
temu [bertemu/ ketemu]	meet
temu [mene-mukan]	find
tenaga nuklir	nuclear energy
tenang	quiet/calm
tenda	tent
tendangan	kick
tengah hari	noon
tengah malam	midnight
tenggorokan	throat
tengkar [bertengkar]	fight
tepat	on time
tepi laut	seaside
tepung	flour
terakhir	last (final)
terbaik	best
terbakar	burnt
terburu-buru	in a hurry
teriak [berteriak]	shout
terima [menerima]	accept
terima kasih	thank you
terjemah [menerje-mahkan]	translate
terka	to guess
terkenal	famous/popular
terlalu	too much/many
terlambat	late (not on time)
termahal	the most expensive
termasuk	included

terminal	station/terminal
teropong	binoculars
tersenyum [senyum]	to smile
tersesat	lost
tertawa	laugh
tertunda	delay
terus	straight ahead
terus terang	honest
tetangga	neighbour
tetap	permanent
tetapi	but
tiap-tiap	each
tiba	to come/arrive
tidak	no/not
tidak ada	neither
tidak ada apa-apa	nothing
tidak aman	unsafe

Tidak apa apa.
No worries. • Never mind.

tidak boleh	not possible
tidak dapat dimengerti	incomprehensible
tidak termasuk	excluded
tidak langsung	non-direct
tidak masuk akal	nonsense
tidak pernah	never
tidak satu pun	none

Tidak usah.
No need.

tidur	asleep/sleep
tikar	mat
tikus	mouse
tikus besar	rat
timur	east
tinggal	to live • exist • stay
tinggi	high • steep • tall
tingkat	floor (storey) • level
tingkat kehidupan	standard of living
tinjauan	review
tinju	boxing
tipis	thin
tisu	tissues • toilet paper
titip [menitipkan]	to deposit (luggage)
TNI (Tentara Nasional Indonesia)	armed forces
toko	shop
toko buku	bookshop
toko oleh-oleh	souvenir shop
toko sepatu	shoe shop
toko serba ada	department stores
tolak [menolak]	refuse
tolong [menolong]	help

Tolong!
Help!

tonton [menonton]	watch
topeng	mask (face)
topi	hat
toples	jar
tua	old (person)
Tuan	Mr/Sir

tugas	duty
Tuhan	God
tukang	skilled craftsperson
tukang cukur rambut	barber
tukang potret	photographer
tukang sihir	magician
tukar [menukarkan]	exchange
tulang	bone
tuli	deaf
tulis [menulis]	write
tumbuh-tumbuhan	vegetation
tunangan	fiancé(e)
tunawisma	homeless
tunggu [menunggu]	wait
tunjuk [menunjuk]	show
turis	tourist
tutup [menutup]	closed/shut

U

uang	money
uang sokongan	dole
uap	steam
ucap [mengucapkan]	mention/express
udang	shrimp
udara	air
ujian	test (exam)
ukiran kayu	woodcarving
ukuran	size (of anything)
ulang [mengulangi]	repeat
ular	snake
ulung	excellent
umum	general
umur	age
ungu	purple
untuk	for
untung	luck/profit
urat darah	vein
usulan	proposal
utama	main
utara	north

W

waktu	when (in the past)
waktu ini	present (time)
waktu makan siang	lunchtime
waktu nanti	when (in the future)
walikota	mayor
wanita	woman/female
waria	transsexual/transvestite
warna	colour
wartawan	journalist
wartel	telephone office
warung	food stall
wasit	referee
wawancara	interview
wayang ...	... puppet
kulit	leather
golek	wooden
WC umum	public toilet
wilayah	region
wol	wool

Y

ya	yes
Yahudi	Jewish
yang	which
yang berikutnya	next
yang lalu	ago • past (before)

Yuk!
Come on!

Z

zakar	penis

INDEX

INDEX

FINDER

Phrasebooks

Lonely Planet phrasebooks are packed with essential words and phrases to help travellers communicate with the locals. With colour tabs for quick reference, an extensive vocabulary and use of script, these handy pocket-sized language guides cover day-to-day travel situations.

- handy pocket-sized books
- easy to understand Pronunciation chapter
- clear & comprehensive Grammar chapter
- romanisation alongside script to allow ease of pronunciation
- script throughout so users can point to phrases for every situation
- full of cultural information and tips for the traveller

'...vital for a real DIY spirit and attitude in language learning'

– Backpacker

'the phrasebooks have good cultural backgrounders and offer solid advice for challenging situations in remote locations'

– San Francisco Examiner

Arabic (Egyptian) • Arabic (Moroccan) • Australian *(Australian English, Aboriginal and Torres Strait languages)* • Baltic States *(Estonian, Latvian, Lithuanian)* • Bengali • Brazilian • Burmese • British • Cantonese • Central Asia • Central Europe *(Czech, French, German, Hungarian, Italian, Slovak)* • Eastern Europe *(Bulgarian, Czech, Hungarian, Polish, Romanian, Slovak)* • Ethiopian (Amharic) • Fijian • French • German • Greek • Hill Tribes • Hindi/Urdu • Indonesian • Italian • Japanese • Korean • Lao • Latin American Spanish • Malay • Mandarin • Mediterranean Europe *(Albanian, Croatian, Greek, Italian, Macedonian, Maltese, Serbian, Slovene)* • Mongolian • Nepali • Papua New Guinea • Pilipino (Tagalog) • Quechua • Russian • Scandinavian Europe *(Danish, Finnish, Icelandic, Norwegian, Swedish)* • South-East Asia *(Burmese, Indonesian, Khmer, Lao, Malay, Tagalog Pilipino, Thai, Vietnamese)* • Spanish (Castilian) *(also includes Catalan, Galician and Basque)* • Sri Lanka • Swahili • Thai • Tibetan • Turkish • Ukrainian • USA *(US English, Vernacular, Native American languages, Hawaiian)* • Vietnamese • Western Europe *(Basque, Catalan, Dutch, French, German, Greek, Irish)*

COMPLETE LIST OF LONELY PLANET BOOKS

AFRICA Africa – the South • Africa on a shoestring • Arabic (Egyptian) phrasebook • Arabic (Moroccan) phrasebook • Cairo • Cape Town • Central Africa • East Africa • Egypt • Egypt travel atlas • Ethiopian (Amharic) phrasebook • The Gambia & Senegal • Kenya • Kenya travel atlas • Malawi, Mozambique & Zambia • Morocco • North Africa • South Africa, Lesotho & Swaziland • South Africa, Lesotho & Swaziland travel atlas • Swahili phrasebook • Trekking in East Africa • Tunisia • West Africa • Zimbabwe, Botswana & Namibia • Zimbabwe, Botswana & Namibia travel atlas
Travel Literature: The Rainbird: A Central African Journey • Songs to an African Sunset: A Zimbabwean Story • Mali Blues: Traveling to an African Beat

AUSTRALIA & THE PACIFIC Australia • Australian phrasebook • Bushwalking in Australia • Bushwalking in Papua New Guinea • Fiji • Fijian phrasebook • Islands of Australia's Great Barrier Reef • Melbourne • Micronesia • New Caledonia • New South Wales & the ACT • New Zealand • Northern Territory • Outback Australia • Papua New Guinea • Papua New Guinea (Pidgin) phrasebook • Queensland • Rarotonga & the Cook Islands • Samoa • Solomon Islands • South Australia • Sydney • Tahiti & French Polynesia • Tasmania • Tonga • Tramping in New Zealand • Vanuatu • Victoria • Western Australia
Travel Literature: Islands in the Clouds • Sean & David's Long Drive

CENTRAL AMERICA & THE CARIBBEAN Bahamas and Turks & Caicos • Barcelona • Bermuda • Central America on a shoestring • Costa Rica • Cuba • Dominican Republic & Haiti • Eastern Caribbean • Guatemala, Belize & Yucatán: La Ruta Maya • Jamaica • Mexico • Mexico City • Panama
Travel Literature: Green Dreams: Travels in Central America

EUROPE Amsterdam • Andalucía • Austria • Baltic States phrasebook • Berlin • Britain • British phrasebook • Central Europe • Central Europe phrasebook • Croatia • Czech & Slovak Republics • Denmark • Dublin • Eastern Europe • Eastern Europe phrasebook • Edinburgh • Estonia, Latvia & Lithuania • Europe • Finland • France • French phrasebook • Germany • German phrasebook • Greece • Greek phrasebook • Hungary • Iceland, Greenland & the Faroe Islands • Ireland • Italian phrasebook • Italy • Lisbon • London • Mediterranean Europe • Mediterranean Europe phrasebook • Paris • Poland • Portugal • Portugal travel atlas • Prague • Provence & the Côte D'Azur • Romania & Moldova • Russia, Ukraine & Belarus • Russian phrasebook • Scandinavian & Baltic Europe • Scandinavian Europe phrasebook • Scotland • Slovenia • Spain • Spanish phrasebook • St Petersburg • Switzerland • Trekking in Spain • Ukrainian phrasebook • Vienna • Walking in Britain • Walking in Italy • Walking in Ireland • Walking in Switzerland • Western Europe • Western Europe phrasebook
Travel Literature: The Olive Grove: Travels in Greece

INDIAN SUBCONTINENT Bangladesh • Bengali phrasebook • Bhutan • Delhi • Goa • Hindi/Urdu phrasebook • India • India & Bangladesh travel atlas • Indian Himalaya • Karakoram Highway • Nepal • Nepali phrasebook • Pakistan • Rajasthan • South India • Sri Lanka • Sri Lanka phrasebook • Trekking in the Indian Himalaya • Trekking in the Karakoram & Hindukush • Trekking in the Nepal Himalaya

COMPLETE LIST OF LONELY PLANET BOOKS

Travel Literature: In Rajasthan • Shopping for Buddhas

ISLANDS OF THE INDIAN OCEAN Madagascar & Comoros • Maldives • Mauritius, Réunion & Seychelles

MIDDLE EAST & CENTRAL ASIA Arab Gulf States • Central Asia • Central Asia phrasebook • Iran • Israel & the Palestinian Territories • Israel & the Palestinian Territories travel atlas • Istanbul • Jerusalem • Jordan & Syria • Jordan, Syria & Lebanon travel atlas • Lebanon • Middle East on a shoestring • Turkey • Turkish phrasebook • Turkey travel atlas • Yemen
Travel Literature: The Gates of Damascus • Kingdom of the Film Stars: Journey into Jordan

NORTH AMERICA Alaska • Backpacking in Alaska • Baja California • California & Nevada • Canada • Florida • Hawaii • Honolulu • Los Angeles • Miami • New England USA • New Orleans • New York City • New York, New Jersey & Pennsylvania • Pacific Northwest USA • Rocky Mountain States • San Francisco • Seattle • Southwest USA • USA • USA phrasebook • Vancouver • Washington, DC & the Capital Region
Travel Literature: Drive Thru America

NORTH-EAST ASIA Beijing • Cantonese phrasebook • China • Hong Kong • Hong Kong, Macau & Guangzhou • Japan • Japanese phrasebook • Japanese audio pack • Korea • Korean phrasebook • Kyoto • Mandarin phrasebook • Mongolia • Mongolian phrasebook • North-East Asia on a shoestring • Seoul • South-West China • Taiwan • Tibet • Tibetan phrasebook • Tokyo
Travel Literature: Lost Japan

SOUTH AMERICA Argentina, Uruguay & Paraguay % Bolivia • Brazil • Brazilian phrasebook • Buenos Aires • Chile & Easter Island • Chile & Easter Island travel atlas • Colombia • Ecuador & the Galapagos Islands • Latin American Spanish phrasebook • Peru • Quechua phrasebook • Rio de Janeiro • South America on a shoestring • Trekking in the Patagonian Andes • Venezuela
Travel Literature: Full Circle: A South American Journey

SOUTH-EAST ASIA Bali & Lombok • Bangkok • Burmese phrasebook • Cambodia • Hill Tribes phrasebook • Ho Chi Minh City • Indonesia • Indonesian phrasebook • Indonesian audio pack • Jakarta • Java • Laos • Lao phrasebook • Laos travel atlas • Malay phrasebook • Malaysia, Singapore & Brunei • Myanmar (Burma) • Philippines • Pilipino (Tagalog) phrasebook • Singapore • South-East Asia on a shoestring • South-East Asia phrasebook • Thailand • Thailand's Islands & Beaches • Thailand travel atlas • Thai phrasebook • Thai audio pack • Vietnam • Vietnamese phrasebook • Vietnam travel atlas

ALSO AVAILABLE: Antarctica • Brief Encounters: Stories of Love, Sex & Travel • Chasing Rickshaws • Not the Only Planet: Travel Stories from Science Fiction • Travel with Children • Traveller's Tales

LONELY PLANET

FREE Lonely Planet Newsletters

We love hearing from you and think you'd like to hear from us.

Planet Talk

Our FREE quarterly printed newsletter is full of tips from travellers and anecdotes from Lonely Planet guidebook authors. Every issue is packed with up-to-date travel news and advice, and includes:

- a postcard from Lonely Planet co-founder Tony Wheeler
- a swag of mail from travellers
- a look at life on the road through the eyes of a Lonely Planet author
- topical health advice
- prizes for the best travel yarn
- news about forthcoming Lonely Planet events
- a complete list of Lonely Planet books and other titles

To join our mailing list, residents of the UK, Europe and Africa can email us at go@lonelyplanet.co.uk; residents of North and South America can email us at info@lonelyplanet.com; the rest of the world can email us at talk2us@lonelyplanet.com.au, or contact any Lonely Planet office.

LONELY PLANET OFFICES

Australia
PO Box 617, Hawthorn,
Victoria 3122
☎ (03) 9819 1877
fax (03) 9819 6459
email: talk2us@lonelyplanet.com.au

USA
150 Linden St, Oakland,
CA 94607
☎ (510) 893 8555
TOLL FREE: 800 275 8555
fax (510) 893 8572
email: info@lonelyplanet.com

UK
10a Spring Place,
London NW5 3BH
☎ (020) 7428 4800
fax (020) 7428 4828
email: go@lonelyplanet.co.uk

France
1 rue du Dahomey, 75011 Paris
☎ 01 55 25 33 00
fax 01 55 25 33 01
email: bip@lonelyplanet.fr

World Wide Web: www.lonelyplanet.com ***or*** **AOL keyword: lp**
Lonely Planet Images: lpi@lonelyplanet.com.au